The Vulnerable Man

Break your patterns
Master your emotions
Reclaim your life

THOMAS ANDERSON

THE VULNERABLE MAN

Reclaim your life

Master your emotions

Break your patterns

TRIGNITE

Contents

CHAPTER 1

Introduction

"*I might as well kill myself, that's what I've been thinking.*" This is what I wrote in my diary in July 2015. The idea of suicide came and went, as it had done for years. When I was in my darkest place, these thoughts came at night and I made plans to make it look like an accident. It had to be that way because I am a person who is always trying to help others, and suicide wouldn't allow my family to benefit from my life insurance. So, how to do it? Fall off a bridge and drown? Perhaps a car accident?

I never spoke to anyone about these thoughts—I mean, what would they think of me, that I was mentally ill. I think that there are a lot of us out there harboring thoughts and feelings that we don't talk about. We construct a wall to hide behind because we are afraid to show who we really are. This wall can stop us from learning how to handle and understand our emotions and feelings. We get stuck in an "emotional prison," either paralyzed, depressed, seeking different avenues of escape, or acting out, triggered by different situations. We live in a society where we are supposed to be strong; we mustn't let our feelings show or be vulnerable and perceived as weak—and this might be especially so for men. The last few years of my life have been transformative; I have broken old patterns and I have discovered and understood more about myself. I have seen how my fear of sharing my feelings and being myself has held me back, and I have come to realize that through the years I started playing roles, and not being truly myself. Nowadays I understand and handle the emotions and feelings that arise in different situations, they don't stop me from being myself anymore. I have found the way back to myself and I possess an inner strength and security in being the person I have always been underneath. I have opened the way for the real Thomas to emerge again, and I can consciously manage my feelings and thoughts in a new way, every day. I have come to realize how important it is to be able to talk openly about the state of your life in the moment, how you feel, the thoughts you have. To do that, we need to create a more emotionally safe society in which it is okay to be vulnerable. Imagine a society where it is okay to talk about a painful relationship, an illness in the family, your own stress, your anxiety about not being good enough, or your thoughts of suicide. That is what I mean by emotionally safe, an environment or society in which it is safe to express emotions, all of them. By better understanding and expressing what we feel and experience, we will understand each other better. And when we better understand ourselves and others, we can solve disagreements and problems more easily, without offensive or defensive behavior or drama. It strengthens and deepens our relationships and allows us to live more wholeheartedly. With this book, I want to share my journey, and it is my hope that it will help pave the way for new thoughts and a climate in which we all have the courage to openly share and talk about our feelings. Then we can break free from our emotional prisons and get a better understanding for each other, thereby creating a more compassionate society.

By being boldly vulnerable, we can let go of old and limiting "truths" and thereby open up for a broader perspective of affection, openness and tolerance. Being vulnerable is about being honest with ourselves and our history, about sharing how we feel and what we think, and about sharing our journey as human beings, because no matter how alone we might feel when things are tough—we are more similar than we think. I learned this when I was brave enough to open up, and it made me a stronger person. And so I want to share my journey, because it is a story that I think most people can relate to, in some way at least. And I hope that I can be a companion to help you along your own path to bold vulnerability. My goal is to share my experiences and reflections, and I hope that the book will be a guide on your journey to change, as well as a friend who exemplifies how it feels to go through change, with the thoughts, the worries, the doubts. It is hard to break old patterns, hard to break out of that emotional prison and take those first steps towards the life you want. I know because I have done it. And now, as you make your own journey, I will do it again, walking alongside you as you read the book.

The message in this book is important for everyone but it might be of extra significance to men, because men are not as used to understanding and sharing their feelings as women. And it is my firm belief—indeed my experience—that there are a lot of men out there who wished they could open up and share their thoughts and pain in a constructive way. But society's norms stop us from doing this. Therefore, we must change those norms. We men must take responsibility—for our children, for our partners, for our friends, for ourselves, and for society. We must show, each and every one of us, that being vulnerable and sensitive is not the same thing as being weak. It is being human.

When I was in my darkest place, I learned about the HSP genetic trait and what it means to be a *Highly Sensitive Person*. This was an eye opener and a turning point for me, and I began to better understand my feelings and emotions. It also helped me put my feelings and thoughts into words—all those things that I thought made me "wrong" and "different" were right there, described as parts of the HSP trait. It made me feel less alone and I began to listen more to myself and trust myself. It made me understand my own reactions to different situations and stimuli. It made me see that we absorb and process impressions differently—it was not that I was wrong, I just saw things differently. It also gave me a deeper understanding of my own sensitivity, helped me truly allow myself to be who I am, and gave me perspective and a re-evaluation of my earlier experiences. Many books, for example about HSP, have had an influence on my thoughts and perspective. In a "menu" at the end of this book, you will find the books that have been the most important to me. Aside from reading, I have found support and tools in leadership courses, individual coaching, and yoga retreats for highly sensitive persons.

While I don't want to go too deeply into any theories here, I think that you will get a better feel for my book if you know a little about highly sensitive persons. HSP is not a new clinical diagnosis, it is an innate personality trait with which you can identify to varying degrees. The term was coined by psychologist Elaine N. Aron, who has conducted research in the field of *sensory processing sensitivity* (SPS) since 1991. A person who has this trait is called a highly sensitive person, and has a more sensitive nervous system, is more attentive to their environment, and processes more information. I think that Aron's abbreviation *DOES* describes this in a good way. The D stands for Depth of Processing, i.e. that you take in more information and process it on a deeper level. This has to do with everything from the mood in a room, the manner in which someone says something, sounds, smells, and so on. The O stands for Overstimulation, a situation in which your mind gets exhausted and your body doesn't function at full capacity. Because you take in more information and process it on a deeper level, you will likely become overstimulated and exhausted more quickly in various situations. For example: you are visiting a new city with your family, you have been out and about all day and you are completely exhausted from all the sensory input. You have no energy left in the evening, when all of you are supposed to go out for dinner. Everyone else seems to up for it though (because they haven't absorbed so much input), so you feel bad because you "ruin the evening for the others." The E stands for Emotional Reactivity, i.e. an increased empathic ability. You perceive more signals from other people and can therefore more easily identify with their mood. This is obviously a good thing, but it can also mean that you confuse your own feelings with those of other people. The S stands for Sensing the Subtle, which means sensing the things that are not spoken, or subtle signals that other people can't sense. This was a very short description of the HSP trait, and if you want to learn more about it there is a lot of information online—but I highly recommend Elaine N. Aron's books on the subject. Aron estimates that around 15–20 % of the population are highly sensitive, so it is definitely something that is worth investigating further.

In this book, you will follow me on my personal journey over three years. I have kept a diary for many years, and I now share it openly so that you can follow my inner feelings and thoughts. Perhaps you can identify with these thoughts and if you do, I hope that you will talk to someone about whatever emerges. The reason for my openness is that I have felt that it has been easier to open my heart when I have heard other people's stories. We are not alone with our thoughts, feelings, and fears. Others have been through similar experiences, and they probably have the same need to share as you do. When I heard other people's stories, I realized that I wasn't alone. It gave me the courage to finally put the things that were stirring up inside me into words. I hope that my words will help you reach the same realization and inspire you to invite more of yourself into your life. I am okay the way I am, and so are you.

CHAPTER 2

What You Need to Know About Me Before You Read My Diary

Hi, my name is Thomas Anderson. I have kept a diary for 18 years. Or my "book for write-keen days" as I call it. Now you get an early glimpse of who I am—I don't want to call it a diary because the duty, the demand, and the pressure of writing every day doesn't sit well with me. It is a book for when I feel like writing, when it feels right and easy and there is no pressure. I have always felt a little different, like I don't really fit into the male norm. It is as if I think and talk differently. I have never had the proper "male" interests. I feel anxiety about what other people think. I want to challenge myself and accomplish a lot, but afterwards I feel completely drained. My mood swings up and down in a way I don't understand. And then, with the insight that I am a highly sensitive person and that it is okay to feel like this, everything falls into place.

I have a Master of Science in Industrial Engineering and Management. I have succeeded in my professional life; I have challenged myself and taken on interesting jobs and assignments that have taken me a long way. Among other things, I have been a project manager for global projects at a multinational company. Through the years I have partaken in many different activities and I have always been committed: handball, student orchestra, student pub, class parent, my band. I have always been an outgoing person and I have many friends. But somewhere there has always been an emptiness, because for a long time I lacked that close friend with whom I could share everything. Now that I, after much doubt and pondering, am writing this book, I am not the same man I was three years ago. Back then, I thought I had overcome my obstacles, and I had everything a "successful and happy man" is supposed to have: wife and children (albeit stepchildren), a well-paid and challenging job, a nice house… Now, I am single, live in an apartment, and run my own business. But I have probably never felt better than I do today.

I grew up in a small village in Dalarna, a province in the middle of Sweden. It was an idyllic village with a population of around eight hundred, and my elementary school had about seventy students. When I started junior high school, I had to take the bus to the nearest town, the old mining town of Grängesberg. The closest high school was in Ludvika, even farther away. It felt like a big place, but its population was only about 15,000. In high school, I was into both sports and music. I got hooked on handball, which was big in Ludvika back then; I appreciated playing team sport and my friends there. At age ten I began to play the saxophone, and music has followed me ever since. I feel good when I am in different orchestras and on stage playing. I graduated with good grades from both middle school and high school.

After my university studies in the city of Linköping, I moved to Gothenburg in 2004 when I got a job at Volvo, and I still live there. With a population of 600,000, Gothenburg is Sweden's second largest city, located on the west coast. I built up my career, rose through the organization, and I liked the tough jobs at work. I also got the opportunity to take various leadership courses, which made me reflect more about group dynamics, who I am, and how others perceive me. Before taking those leadership courses I had just kept going, taking on everything and enjoying the challenges. I knew that I excelled at work, but there was still a gnawing feeling that something was not right. This feeling was recurrent; sometimes it told me not to do certain things. But as an engineer and a logical person, I thought that feelings were not something worth listening to; they are not logical. So I pushed them away and kept going. Today, I know that I have to listen to those feelings.

In the spring of 2009, I met a fantastic girl, whom I call "C" in this book. We connected instantly and became good friends, and about a year later that friendship had developed into something more. Then came the thoughts. What happens now, are we going to be a couple? She had three children from an earlier relationship—how would that work? The practical and logical Thomas thought, "Isn't it better to meet someone without kids?" At first, I backed away from the relationship, but my feelings for C were too strong and I listened to them. In 2011 we moved in together, bought a house together and I became a stepfather to three boys every other week. It felt absolutely right, and I entered the relationship with positive energy and a commitment to fix up the house and get to know the boys. Both me and C had interesting jobs and were focused on our careers. At about the same time as we bought the house, I left Volvo and began working as a Management Consultant, taking on new challenges. Our family grew with the addition of two wonderful cats. Everything was as it should be, everyday life as a parent and all that goes with it. Leaving and picking up the kids at daycare. All the activities with the kids, our own activities. We got married in 2013 and had everything one is supposed to have. I liked my role at work and at home, the role of father. There was a lot going on all the time, but that was as it should be. But then something began to change, I started to get tired, grumpy, things were not fun anymore. What was wrong with me, I lived a good life…

CHAPTER 3

The Road to Burnout
Is Paved with Good Intentions

Wednesday, December 31, 2014

*And so it's New Year's Eve, the last day of the year, a year filled with
events. Christmas was good with everyone here, the boys were with us so
on Christmas Eve we were nine people here. The boys left for their father's
on Monday, so now C and I have a little time to ourselves, just us and
the cats. It's nice to have some time off, I feel like it's been a lot before the
holidays, and then I got the flu on the last week, I still worked a little even
though I should've stayed at home. So, I was a bit tired over Christmas.
Unfortunately, I couldn't go with the others to my father-in-law's on the
20th, I had to stay at home and rest.*

*Then I feel that even though it's been a couple of really good days, it's a
lot with all the people around. I'm often bad at taking time off for myself.
Instead I try to do stuff for everyone else and forget about myself, classic
Thomas… During the last couple of days, I've felt restless, a little grumpy,
tired, I want to do stuff and at the same time I don't. I took a walk today
and felt like my head was empty and I couldn't think. I think that's it. I need
to rest but I can't find peace. That's why I need to move my body, then take
it easy, socialize when I have the energy for it. Hang out with people who
give me energy. It feels so weird when we've been together talking and I've
been there but I've felt empty, like I should talk more or give more, but I*

haven't known what to say. But it's okay just to be there. Yes, I have to think about that, how to create a break for myself without putting the responsibility on others. I need to find my rest and my way of charging my batteries.

It has in any case been a very good year. I've met friends, managed a guys' weekend in Copenhagen with the guys from Linköping. And I've done well at my job, almost reached my sales target. I've received very positive critique from my boss, the regional vice manager and the regional manager. Got an award in our group at the Christmas party. It feels very good that everything's going well and that I'm getting good results. It's a lot of fun and I'm growing as a person. It's a lot of sales, customer contact, seminars, launching new projects with our clients, finding opportunities, getting client responsibilities, working on deals. It's all very educational and fun, and I hope it continues next year and that everything keeps going in the same direction.

Now it's time to make New Year's food! I'll be back!

I have always enjoyed having a lot to do. I like to fix things and I love to commit myself and be there for others. Prior to this diary entry, I normally had time to myself; I didn't have to think about and understand the quiet that I needed. On New Year's Eve 2014, I had been in a new role for a couple of years, as a husband, with a house, stepchildren and a new job. I enjoyed helping out around the house and at work, and I always had enough energy to do it all. I enjoyed the role as stepfather. I fixed things in the house that needed fixing. I had a new extended family with a mother-in-law, father-in-law, sister-in-law, the kids' father and his partner. I took the kids to school and met other parents, I went to handball, soccer and met all the parents there too. And I wanted to be there because it was fun. I liked being married, I supported my wife and I was there for her like she was there for me. I put a lot of effort into my career and I had a new position which I felt comfortable in and which included many interesting meetings and new opportunities; I wanted to bring my A-game and I had exciting challenges to tackle.

There were lots of different things to do all the time, but I failed to make time for myself, for reflection and recovery. I didn't see or think that those natural breaks I had earlier in life were something I actually needed. And now that there were things to do all the time—how could I say that I just wanted to do nothing?

Tuesday, January 20, 2015

Yesterday was my birthday and I have reached the venerable age of 37 ☺ Tonight I've done yoga and some reading. C and the kids are watching Friends.

It feels as if a lot of thoughts keep spinning round, so I figured I'd write a bit. I've felt a little tired and blue over the last couple of weeks, like I'm empty, as if no one really likes me. I want to do stuff but can't think of anything that I feel like doing, I've felt cranky and I take things the wrong way, say nothing but I guess people can tell anyway. It's tough. I know that I can influence the way I feel, that I create my own happiness, and yet this happens. I have wonderful stepchildren who love me, good friends who like me, good colleagues, we're healthy, the cats are healthy. Everything is fine and yet it's not. Met Lovisa on the bus today, she said I should take extra vitamin D, that you need it when it's so dark outside. Perhaps I should try that because I'm usually tired in the fall and winter.

Yes, it's a bit weird, but still it feels like things are getting better. The toughest feeling is when I feel that I want to be positive but I can't, don't have the energy. If we're going over to friends, for example, I just don't want to, can't say why, but I just want to stay at home and not socialize. But then I want to meet people anyway… It's a bit sad, sometimes I want to be social and sometimes it's just yuck…

Perhaps it's just a matter of attitude, since most of the time things work out well. Feels like I'm sometimes negative when someone asks me. Like I'm a slow starter but everything works out eventually. I should wait a little before I answer, so I have time to think… I have so many little thoughts… But now it's time for bed, I'll see where it lands… ☺

It seems so obvious now, in retrospect, but I didn't understand then that for a long time I had been teetering on the edge of "burnout." During this time, I was tired and grumpy, I wanted to do things and yet I didn't, I got stuck in a weird routine, I wanted to be happy but didn't have the energy, and I punished myself. I didn't understand myself; I lacked the self-awareness and tools needed to make time for myself, time I needed in my everyday life. With a relationship and a family, the "me-time" that came naturally before disappeared; I placed expectations on myself regarding how one should be in a relationship, and that meant cutting away my me-time because I didn't understand how much I needed it. I think this is probably not uncommon. We all probably have an idea of how to behave in a relationship, an idea that we get from our parents, friends, the norms of society, and the media. What we don't see is how our role models act when they aren't in the limelight, how they recover, how they feel behind the scenes. Naturally, we have different ways to relax and recover, and differing needs of me-time. One partner in a relationship might need more time to process the day's events. Just because I want to be alone or need time for my thoughts to settle, it doesn't mean that I am rejecting other people—I just need a little time to myself. I didn't understand that then, I just wanted to always be there for everyone else, when I really should have expressed my own needs in a way that was not open for interpretation.

I now understand that I have been in situations before where there has simply been too much stimulus. I have become overstimulated, and the pattern is an old one even if I didn't know what it was all about at the time. Back then I would be full of energy and fill my calendar with things, and then it would just become too much; my energy would be drained and there was no me-time. And I would feel weird, because my calendar was filled with fun things, but they felt like obligations. Especially come August and September, I would usually be full of energy, booking up the entire fall. Then, in October and November, I would be so tired and regret putting so much in the calendar. I would then begin to make sure I had free weekends with nothing booked in, because I would feel stressed out and unable to enjoy my weekends if I knew that I was fully booked a month ahead—even if all the stuff booked in was fun.

I think that when you are full of energy and have a lot of fun one weekend, you want to have just as much fun the next—and soon, your calendar is full. There is also a social norm that puts expectations on us; we are supposed to want to get together and spend time with family, relatives, and friends. If you don't speak to or see each other in a while, you feel guilty. And if you are a conscientious person like me and want to commit to whatever is planned, it can become stressful to have lots of things in your calendar. It is about the balance between activity and rest, about accelerating or braking. Stress can be seen as always driving at full speed without braking once in a while, and it is the same thing with activities and pleasures. When I am full of energy and driving at full speed, I need to remind myself and be aware of the fact that I am in that energy *right now*, I am at full speed *now*, but I will not always be, and therefore I must make conscious choices when I book things in. Too much of the good stuff without pauses in between makes me unable to enjoy that good stuff, and it can instead become a stress factor. I think many people can identify with this. Of course, you can cancel things that you have booked, but it can be difficult—at least it was for me—because you are supposed to keep your promises...

Sunday, March 29, 2015

It has been up and down lately. One week I'm at full speed and feeling good, the next I'm down and things suck. But I think things are taking shape and falling into place. On the one hand it's work, it can be a lot one week, delivering deals, important meetings. Then the next week it's a lot of waiting and less to do. But during the down weeks I feel like I should do more even though I really ought to take advantage of the calm and do whatever I feel like. But then it feels like it's easier to be fully booked and not have to think about what it is I actually want to do. On the other hand, C has a lot to do, both at work and in her spare time with yoga, dog training courses, etc. So, when I have less to do at work and want to do stuff at home, she is busy and that's tough. It's like I'm not needed, not at home nor at work, but that's not true—it's more about doing what I feel like doing and not expecting anyone else to decide what I should do.

I just got a strong feeling, a little "kick" of insight. I can't put expectations on other people, I need to decide my own way. How easy it is to fall into that, to always please others. Of course, it's good to be helpful but I mustn't forget myself and the things I want.

At this time I found it difficult to have a lot to do at work one week and then very little the next week. I got caught up in fixing things for other people and had a hard time finding peace and quiet when there was actually time for it. And for a long time, I forgot what I needed to do to feel well. As long as I could fix things for others, it was good and I had things "to do" but then, when I had time for myself—what should I do then? I almost felt unhappy about not having anything to do, as if life was not meaningful unless I produced, achieved, and delivered. And I asked myself what I should do with my time. I was eager to please others, but at the same time I needed to change that so that I got more time to myself. But it can be difficult to break away from old patterns. That "kick" of insight was important; I was reminded that *I* needed to change. I am the only one who knows what I need to feel well. I think it is easy to get caught up in fixing things for other people, and it can be something you enjoy. Then, when all of a sudden you get the time to do what you want, it can be hard. You are so used to doing things for others that you have forgotten what you want and what gives you energy.

In the spring of 2015, we began talking about getting a dog. C attended a dog course, and she wanted a dog for the children's sake. They wanted one too. I felt that it was going to be hard, that I couldn't add anything more at that time and that it was going to be a lot of work for me. But I also felt that I didn't want to cause a fuss, and I told myself that it would be alright. So, I didn't trust my feelings, despite my whole body screaming no. Instead I grew quiet, annoyed, but I said okay because I didn't want to fight.

Tuesday, May 5, 2015

Today is a rainy day, I've come home from work and will go to yoga class soon. Today is also a weird day, I feel tired, down and sad. Yesterday I was feeling great… Weird… One thing I think is affecting me is C. She is down and tired right now, had a rough day yesterday and we talked about it. The strange thing is that when we talk, or rather when she talks and I listen, it feels like as soon as she is done, she doesn't want to listen to me. It feels like she just turns off, becomes quiet and then, all of a sudden, becomes angry and firm, ordering that things be done. I realize I might be overreacting a bit, but she becomes curt and distant.

This morning we talked about an After Work on Friday[1]. She has decided to go, and there are several mutual friends going. Yet she says "I'm going" without asking me if I want to go too. I don't know if I feel like going, but it's the sense of her mostly thinking of only herself. If I'm doing something, I usually ask her if she wants to come along, while she goes her own way without asking me. She wants to do her stuff, meet her friends, do yoga, attend her own classes, go on vacation with the kids and a friend but not with me, and she's getting a dog. The question is: What are we supposed to do? I know that I'm also responsible for doing things with my friends, but it all just feels so sad. And then I begin to think that difficult thought, "Perhaps it's over." Aren't we having fun anymore? What's the cause? And everything feels really tough all of a sudden. Then I feel like I can't say all

---

1   In Sweden, lots of bars and restaurants have deals for drinks and food called "After Work," especially on Fridays. Often you pay a set price for cheap drinks and access to a buffet. It is mainly a way for coworkers to get together outside of the workplace, but people who haven't been to work can also enjoy an After Work. The term is also used when going out for a beer after a workday, regardless of weekday and whether there are deals or not.

that to her, because what will happen then—then it might be over for real.
Is that what I want? On the other hand, I know I exaggerate sometimes and
think the worst. But it also feels like I'm good to have around, I fix things
around the house, I take care of the boys, listen when she needs it—but the
way I think and feel is not important, there's no room for that. Maybe I'm
wrong but it's tricky and difficult to discuss. Well, we'll see what happens.
I guess it's a crisis that we will get through one way or another.

I understand now that I am very good at picking up other people's moods
and emotions, and that I also reflect other people's moods easier than
others. In essence, this is a good thing that lets me understand and em-
pathize with other people's situations. But if you are not aware of it, you
will take that energy with you and it can make you feel bad, as the case
was with me. I didn't understand why my mood changed so much, that
it could actually be affected by other people's moods. Maybe it has happened to you too, someone says, "It's so good talking to you, now I feel
much better" and then move on, while you sit there weighing a thousand
tons. You have taken over the other person's emotion and he or she is
relieved for the moment. It is a fantastic skill to have, but you have to be
able to release the emotion afterwards.

As a highly sensitive person, you can feel when a situation is tense
and that someone is feeling down. There is a feeling of malaise because
of their bad mood. In my case, C felt very down, and it was tough. I felt
bad and wanted to fix things, so I took on the responsibility of making
everything okay. But because I didn't understand that I had taken over
her emotions, I made things worse. I tried to solve a problem where C
really needed time and space to herself. I was worried it was something
I had done, that something between us was wrong; I made up disaster
stories in my head and quickly wanted to hear from C that she wasn't
angry with me. I think that many people can identify with this; you feel
that something is wrong, you want to fix it but at the same time you are
a bit lost and worried that *you* have done something wrong.

At the time of this diary entry there was a lot I couldn't say. Why was it like that, why couldn't I express how I felt? I was afraid to mention the things on my mind. I was afraid that if I talked about how I really felt, then C wouldn't like me anymore. I thought that I was being difficult and would perhaps be left out. I didn't want to open myself up to the chaos that might come.

May 5, 2015, continued

We talked and I got things off my chest. It feels great, because it has been a thought monster on my part. I've felt that I'm not good enough, that I always have to give a little more otherwise people won't like me. But why is that, I've got to let it go…

I sometimes ask too many questions when in reality, I want to talk. It can be tiring with too many questions, I enter coaching mode to be there for her. But I must give when I want to give, not give to get in return.

I also feel like people don't want to be near me. It's okay that I'm there to fix things, but when everything is done and it's time for fun, they don't want me there. I mean, I'm just around because I'm necessary, not because they like me…

We talked about difficult things, but it felt good afterwards.

At this time, I felt that things became awkward whenever I was about to talk about emotional stuff. It didn't have to be a difficult question, but I felt pressured and my whole body went rigid. I tensed up, my breathing became shallow, and my brain felt empty. I didn't know what to say, couldn't think, couldn't feel, said nothing except yes or no. But my whole body screamed at me to get out of there. So, I often said yes to what the others wanted. Then, when I got away and began to breathe normally again, the thoughts came: Why did I say that? What do I really want? And at night I thought about what I should have said, or rather how I should go back and change my decision. But—is it okay to change my mind afterwards? Am I weird if I start discussing something we discussed yesterday? (I have noticed that this happens in close relationships and situations of dependency, not in all situations.)

I became nervous, it all felt too much, and I didn't know how to handle disagreements or the fact that we think differently. I was unused to expressing myself, to put what I thought and felt into words. Talking about how I felt brought back memories from my childhood, memories about standing out, of people finding out who I really was. This happened especially if something unexpected or unplanned happened, i.e. when a lot was going on, a lot of information and my brain bubbled with different possibilities and alternatives. I would tense up because I might say something wrong, promise something I would later regret, bare my feelings and be made fun of, or simply because I didn't know the answer right then. After a situation like that, it was easy to think, "Why did I do that, I know what I really want"—but right then, I short-circuited.

I often came back the day after something happened to talk about how I felt or what I should have said. And people would often say to me, "Are you still thinking about that?" And yes, I was. But of course, I made myself feel bad for still thinking about it instead of discussing it right away. I felt like I was being difficult, and why bring up things after such a long time. I should have been able to reply right away.

Sunday, July 5, 2015

It's 10 am, I'm down by Aspholmarna at Saltholmen. I've just had a swim and a cup of coffee. C is at a dog course this weekend so I'm by myself down here. It's been a rough week, some stuff at work, an overdue delivery and the client is very dissatisfied. I realize that I'm taking it very hard and personally. Yesterday didn't feel good at all but things are a bit better now.

A lot has happened since last time. C has quit her job and is on a leave of absence. She began looking for a new job at Christmas and it has affected her a lot the entire spring. When we celebrated her birthday with her family, she told them everything and got 100 % support and confirmation that she's doing the right thing. So on June 1st she handed in her resignation ☺ September 1st is her last day, then she will be free to focus on her dog course, on our dog that will arrive in the middle of July, and she will look into starting her own business with daycare for dogs, courses, etc. It will be exciting to see where it all lands.

Another thing that falls into place is the way I've been feeling. We're not having fun, she's not listening, has no energy. She's been completely drained, given everything at work and it has sapped all her energy. It has made me back away, I have asked her how she's doing, but she's been empty. She's had energy only for her stuff, work, dog course, yoga, friends—and there's been no room for us. With us, I mean the kids and me.

It's all been wrong, and I've grown tired of her not listening. So, during the spring, I've taken many steps back, I don't count on her or expect her to come along to things. I don't expect her to listen… To be interested in what I do, my work, the band, exercise, etc.

I've even thought about a separation, just to get comfortable with the thought. If she just wants to do her own stuff alone, then what is the point of us being together… But as I've said, everything comes into a new light now that she's quit her job and I've told her how I have been pulling away. She understands it and I understand her. But it will still take me a while to come back to the same level of trust. One good thing is that I must think more about what I want. I just booked a week at Herräng[2] to play the saxophone, wanted to do something this summer. We cancelled the hiking trip in the Alps because we're getting a dog. It's mostly C who wants a dog, but I guess I'll enjoy it too. But I feel that I must do my stuff, I need me-time. When C has been away, I have taken on more and more with the kids, forgetting myself—classic Thomas. But now it feels good, I feel stronger and when I thought about breaking up, I thought that everything will be

---

2   Herräng Dance Camp is the world's largest and longest dance festival focusing on the African-American vernacular swing dance tradition. It takes place in Herräng, about an hour's car ride north of Stockholm.

alright, I will find someone. Before, I've thought that everything would go to hell and that I'm worthless. I might as well kill myself, that's what I've been thinking. But I've resolved that and gotten past it with support from my close friend Daniel who says, "You should be Thomas." And now I feel that I am Thomas, and you must like me for who I am or it's not going to work. Yes, it's been a lot, but it feels good that things are getting better even if there are still things left. I need time to myself and we need time together and to have fun again. So, we'll see how things develop.

The thoughts about suicide were recurrent and incredibly difficult. I knew that I would never actually kill myself, but the thoughts were terrible. They often came in the fall when it began to grow darker. They came when I couldn't find a way out, when I felt like I wasn't good enough or that it didn't matter what I did. Sometimes, in my relationship with C, they came when I thought that we might be done, that I wasn't good enough in that role—and I thought about killing myself instead of having to face a breakup. Because I was so afraid and I didn't think I would make it if we broke up. As the caring person that I am, I thought about how to do it so it would look like an accident. Because if it was an accident my family would benefit from my life insurance; they needed the money and the things I did more than me personally, I thought. But then the thoughts went away, and I felt ashamed of even having thought them.

I didn't dare tell anyone about this—what would they think of me then? Who is Thomas who thinks about killing himself, he must be mentally ill. So, it was best to keep it in. The crazy thing is how often this process happened; it happened on several occasions, and I remember thinking, "Okay, here we go again" and it was incredibly tough, but I let the thoughts come. I knew they would pass but it was really hard going through that.

I managed to let go of my suicidal thoughts in several steps. Writing a diary helped me gain perspective as I got to put my thoughts down into words and sentences. I began to question the thoughts about my myself and see the recurrent pattern. What made me feel and think like that at the moment? I also spoke with my friend Daniel about the relationship I was in, how to be myself there, to be Thomas, as he so neatly put it. He helped me remember how things were before and the feeling I had then. Just because a relationship isn't working, it doesn't mean I have to disappear from the face of the earth. And then I used The Journey, a healing method that I studied through Brandon Bay's book *The Journey*. This method in combination with a leadership course and self-revelation taught me to go back to the first memory of an event. In short, you need to find the first awareness of an event that an emotion comes from and let your current self "go back" to that occasion and help your younger self through the emotion you couldn't handle at the time. There are obviously different ways to handle a situation like the one I was in, and this was my way. I tried to go back to the first time I thought about suicide. And I remembered a night on the bus when I was a teenager; I felt sad and dejected about something, I felt worthless but didn't have anyone to talk to. But my grown-up self managed to tell my childhood self that it was okay and that I was there for myself. By finding this event within myself, I realized where the thoughts had originated. It is a part of The Journey to find these situations from which the original emotion comes, and then allow it, understand it, and give yourself the adult advice that you couldn't get at the time. All these steps helped me understand why I had thoughts of suicide, that it was an evil emotional spiral that led to feelings of hopelessness—and through this understanding I could start letting go of the harmful thoughts.

The first time I spoke to others about my thoughts of suicide was at a retreat for highly sensitive persons (I will get back to these retreats later on). And almost all the others said, "We have also had thoughts like that, guess everybody does sometimes." It was so good to finally talk about it and to hear that others had similar thoughts. I was not alone. And then I had a strong feeling of wanting to question the taboo that has been placed upon talking about suicide. Why should it be so difficult to talk about? For me, the thoughts sprung from something that happened, an emotion. So, instead of talking about how wrong it is to take your own life, we should ask why these thoughts enter our heads. What is the underlying emotion? What has happened? Simply talk and share. Remember, I felt that if I told anyone about my suicidal thoughts, they would think I was weird, perhaps even mentally ill. And that stopped me from even mentioning it to the people that I really should have talked to.

For me, it was about feeling lonely, and it went way back. I didn't dare talk about what had happened or what I felt there on the bus when I was a teenager. It had followed me for a long time, that if I felt bad, then I didn't talk about it. It wasn't worth sharing with other people; you are supposed to be happy, bright and positive when you talk to others. The thought of suicide comes when you can't see any other way out. Imagine if we can create an emotionally safe and non-judgmental environment in which we can talk, at an early age. This would obviously benefit everyone, but I think perhaps especially men. Men have a longer way to go. Men are over-represented in suicide statistics. Men are less likely to seek help for mental or physical problems. I think that this has a lot to do with men not being allowed to be vulnerable; we are supposed to be strong and self-reliant—but statistics tell a different story. I have acquaintances who have committed suicide. Perhaps you, the reader, also know someone, or know of someone, who has committed suicide. We often say, "Why didn't they talk about this earlier, why did they keep it all inside?" The pain is hard to endure if it was someone close, and you ask, "Why didn't they talk to me about it?" I think we need to start early, especially us men, to allow ourselves to talk about the difficult things. Our worries. If we feel inadequate. By practicing this and creating an emotionally safe environment, it will feel safer to talk when the tough times come. That is what it is all about—not always talking about difficult things, but *to be allowed to talk when we need to*, and to feel safe enough to talk and receive help.

C and I were having a tough time when we both had so much to do. There was no time to talk and be there for each other. I think I took it personally, which is easy to do whether you are a highly sensitive person or not. I thought that it was all my fault. I thought that our relationship was the problem and that C didn't want to be with me or the family. I didn't dare to talk about my feelings during the spring, because I had no energy. But maybe it wasn't about me or about the relationship not working, but about C being so tired and having so many things affecting her. I didn't know what was right or wrong here, but we had slipped away from each other. Instead of talking and looking at things with perspective, I withdrew and imagined the worst, I sucked it up. But I began to feel hope that we would have more time for each other now that things had changed with her job. But then I ran into problems at work, which took up all of *my* time and energy...

CHAPTER 4

Breaking Patterns

Thursday, July 30, 2015

How these things always come back, not having the courage to do things because they're not perfect. I make things more difficult than they are and dare not believe that anyone really wants to be with me, they just say that to be nice. What is behind this anxiety about not being good enough and people not liking me? It's a pain in the ass to feel like that. Daniel says to me that I should stop playing roles, since I often do that. And I guess that's true.

I sometimes feel that I can become stressed out just from talking to someone, my breathing becomes shallow, I tense up in a weird way. It's odd, somehow I feel responsible for the whole conversation. I take responsibility in many situations, in new groups of people, in new encounters, for the saxophone solo to be perfect, otherwise I'm not good enough. And I think that nobody really wants to have anything to do with me.

It feels like things are happening in my body, like I'm letting go of something, even if it's nothing new but something recurring. But it could be that things go all the way around again and I fall back into the same pattern once more. Especially when there's been a lot of things going on and I can't recharge my batteries and find time to myself.

Another thing that's been on my mind… I don't know how to explain it, but it feels like it is just too much sometimes. There is so much going on in people's thoughts and feelings and it affects me more than I think.

I can be overwhelmed by people who take up too much space, in thought or conversation, and I tense up, lose my energy and drive. I need to work on staying calm when I meet other people, not stress, and separate their energy from my own.

At this point, I was enjoying a week's vacation on my own and I had gone away to play the saxophone. I got a break and time for reflection, and it was clear that I was getting closer to understanding myself and how much I am affected by different stimuli. I reflected on that recurring theme, that I often felt exhausted. I began to understand and see the pattern that emerged: that on the one hand I can be full of energy and hang out with friends and other people, while on the other hand I can be low and feel like I don't fit in. When Daniel told me that I play different roles, I began to understand what he meant: the roles as husband, stepfather, at work and so on. I also felt that I have to be perfect and responsible for many different situations if everything is going to work out. I have always done that; I want to help and be there for other people—it is my fundamental attitude that we are here to help each other. But there is a risk involved with being empathic; you understand how others feel and you want to help, you end up in a sacrificing role where you forget yourself and your own needs. That role—fixing for others, sacrificing yourself and not showing it—brings with it the risk of suffering burnout. And it doesn't show; we don't show it to people we meet, instead we help them with their problems and put up the façade where everything is fine. Then, when we are alone, we can be completely exhausted. And you don't want to be difficult, don't want to make a fuss, just be a helpful person.

I now began to reflect on the patterns I ended up in and the recurring feeling I got when things were tough. What was it that I did to always end up in the same situation and emotion? At this point, I had read a book about so-called schema therapy (*Reinventing Your Life* by Jeffrey E. Young) that I felt influenced my thoughts. (Schema therapy is an offshoot of cognitive behavioral therapy that has been influenced by gestalt therapy and attachment therapy.) The book talks about "lifetraps", that you have a recurring behavior that gets you into the same kind of situation again and again. Even if you end up in a harmful situation, the feeling in your behavior is familiar, which means you follow the familiar behavior and go along with the situation even though it might have negative consequences. In the book, this is exemplified by destructive relationships, substance abuse, and alienation. Many of these habitual behaviors can be traced to our childhood and upbringing. The book also describes how hard it is to break the behavioral pattern. The first thing you have to do is become aware of the pattern and understand what kind of situations you put yourself in.

The book got me to think about what I did, which behaviors I had that put me in situations that were bad for me. What followed me from my childhood? What did I avoid? What role did the norms and expectations of society play? What was habitual and familiar in me that put me in bad situations? Why was I afraid to break these patterns? I read the book during my one-week vacation, and I also spent a lot of time with a couple from Spain whom I got to know. They were people that I liked and also looked up to. We were often together and I felt very relaxed in their company. I was calm, I was myself and didn't play any roles. We had lots of fun together and we talked a lot. On the last evening, the girl said to me, "Thomas, you are a good person." That meant a great deal to me at the time. When I was contemplating patterns, behaviors, and roles, I heard these warm words. These lovely and wonderful people liked me for who I am. How could I get more of that? What did I need to do to change my patterns and thoughts?

I also began to think about how other people affect me, how I pick up on their mood, but at this point I didn't understand what it meant to be a highly sensitive person, or that you can be affected by and absorb other people's emotions. At this point, it just felt weird and "hippy dippy."

Saturday, October 31, 2015

It's been a couple of months since last time and there has been a lot to do at work. A project that has gone wrong and I have been to Stockholm twice to meet an angry client. The managers have been all over me wondering why the project has turned out the way it has. It's been a couple of rough weeks. And apart from that project, I have new projects starting up, deliveries, sales plans, and budget. In August and September, the weekends were busy too with five gigs in six weeks, and I was also away at work over one weekend. Right, and a dog that wakes up early in the mornings. So it's not strange that I've been completely exhausted since mid-October… and I really mean exhausted; I haven't felt like seeing anyone, at work I've just soldiered on, the job has been on my mind on weekends and evenings, it's been two intense months. I'm still beaten, feel that I have to take it easy and just be alone.

You can tell that it's autumn again, as I have so many thoughts. On the one hand, I'm restless, I want something to happen and I want to meet people. On the other hand, I just want to be alone. I feel like I get in the way, that people don't really like me and all that, it comes back somehow.

Talked to C about it yesterday and I said that maybe I should pause for a moment, enjoy work, reap the results. Spend time with colleagues, be the expert, do fun things and not just move on with a feeling of stress. But when I think of it, maybe my colleagues feel done with me and just want me to move on… Wow, that's tough, it's easier to move on to something new than to stay… I wonder if that's the case, is that why I fix a lot—because I don't want people to really get to know me? That people only like me for the things I do and if I don't deliver then nobody wants me. Mm, maybe that's part of it, take it easier, make room in my calendar for colleagues and friends. I don't have to stress and feel that I have to deliver something big and new or that I have to work myself to death to be liked. It's time to pause, enjoy, and be available and open for whatever comes. Mm, I think that's it… exciting. I'll have to come back to that.

This was an incredibly difficult time, but I didn't let anyone know, I just soldiered on. Things were extremely stressful at work; it felt as if everything was being ripped away from me, everything I had built up. I was being questioned, I got insufficient support from management, the client was very angry, and I didn't know what to say during the client meetings. I judged myself very harshly and thought things like, "Why didn't I see this earlier?"; "I should have seen it coming" and "I suck." At the same time, I had other clients with whom everything was fine, and I kept working with them.

I also remember that I used to check my email whenever I had the chance; on the tram, between meetings, in the mornings when I woke up, before I went to bed. In the six weeks when my band had five gigs, late Fridays and Saturdays, I also had to deliver on stage. But I checked my work email between the soundcheck and the gig. I clearly remember the stress with my phone, checking my email, seeing if anything had happened and thinking I should reply right away. I believe that the constant availability we face today poses a problem that we haven't learned to handle. On my part, I meant well, I wanted to be able to help, but at this time I did too much, stretched myself too thin, and didn't prioritize my own recovery. I was unable to put up boundaries; I was always connected and available. I couldn't keep myself from checking my email, Facebook and other social media. And I don't think I am alone in this. I was always connected, never relaxed—and how should I handle that when I am a person who absorbs so much information? This is a relatively new situation. I got my first smartphone in 2011; before that, I had to connect my laptop to have access to my email. Meaning that before 2011 I could choose when I wanted to check my email—now, people could reach me wherever I was. And at this time, I used to check my email before I went to bed in the evenings and when I got up in the mornings, and sometimes reading emails in the evenings could create anxiety: "I have to answer this tomorrow, how should I respond, I wonder what they think." Imagine the difference in sleep quality if I had seen the same email in the morning, when I had arrived in the office! I could have slept with good conscience and would have solved the problem in the same way, instead of worrying and having difficulty sleeping because my thoughts were racing. It is illogical to think that we are being good or productive when we check our email at 11 pm instead of having "working hours" for our email too, and not let it intrude on our spare time and recovery time. We think that we are gaining something by doing that, but are we in fact losing? Nowadays, we need to practice relaxing and disconnecting, but that can actually be a stress factor in itself.

During the fall, it was not only my work that felt difficult and stressful. Unforeseen small things disrupted my rhythm and turned into big, insurmountable problems. I was grumpy and nothing was fun anymore. Afterwards, I could clearly see that I was suffering from burnout. But I didn't let anyone see it, not even C—instead I kept up my façade when meeting people. I delivered on stage, so to speak. But when I was alone, I was completely exhausted. I didn't look for any help, medical or otherwise, and I didn't go on sick leave. As a man, as an engineer, as a person who was used to juggling a lot at once, I didn't admit to myself that I was burned out. I said that I was stressed, that a lot was happening— possibly, I said as much as that I had something similar to burnout (but I still kept it to myself). I thought that it would probably pass, it would get better, I just needed to get over the bump. With the perspective and experience I have today, I realize what difference it could have made if I had been brave enough to expose myself, be vulnerable and talk openly about how I felt, that I felt so tired and inadequate. On the other hand: without the burnout and everything that followed in its wake, I might not have gained the insights I possess today. But I am getting ahead of myself—let us go back to the fall of 2015.

Saturday, November 7, 2015

Today I feel a little philosophical or something. I also feel a bit sluggish, detached, like I just do things. It's been intense lately and I've tried to take it a bit slower. It's worked but there's still something that doesn't feel right. It's a kind of hopelessness and pointlessness, why do I do the things I do? I work hard and get things done both at work and at home, but why? Have I lost sight of what I want to do? What is it that I want? Am I only doing things for other people and not for myself? Sometimes I feel like just going away, taking a break from everything and just... be. Get away from all the musts, all the doing, pushing forward, worrying about failure, worrying about letting people down. If I fail, I'll never get to do anything fun again, what if they discover that I'm a fraud. That's how I think sometimes, and it's tough.

It's difficult to put the emotion into words, but it's persistent, and I feel that I'm only needed if I do things for other people—and if I don't, then I'm not needed anymore. And then I realize that I put myself in those situations when I have lots to do, because then I skip lunches with others, skip the coffee break, just want to be alone. It's a tricky thing...

I sometimes feel like a little boy again, the others wouldn't let me in, wouldn't let me participate. But was that really the case? I just realized that perhaps I seek out a group of people where I don't really belong instead of just staying where I am. Can that be true?

And I think that perhaps it's the same now, I want to go away from work and everything, far away and then start a new job—but maybe that's exactly what I shouldn't do. Maybe what I should do is to stop and do what I want instead of being ambitious and doing what my bosses want. I should go my own way, do the things I believe in, have more time for my colleagues, and have more fun. Yes, I'll do that, it feels right. I need energy for other things than work.

I should pause, listen, follow my feeling, and enjoy life. Don't stress! I get stressed when I feel like I'm not good enough—I have to realize that I am good enough. I've done so much this year and learned a lot!! And things are good at home, I'm there for my family, C gets her own time and grows through her own things. The kids are doing good, Mom, Dad, and my brother are good, and yet I feel like I'm not good enough. Let go of the pretensions and be who you are!! It shouldn't be that hard! I mean, of course it's easy, just do it, let go… I'm doing it!!!

I stayed behind after a yoga session led by my friend Lovisa. As we put the yoga mats and other equipment away, I mentioned that I was tired at work and that there was just so much all the time. And she said to me, "You yourself have to prioritize your time; you have to say no when you have enough." And she told me to say to my colleagues, "I have these three things here, and I want to deliver them with quality, so I can't do anything else right now." That was an expression that I felt was really helpful—and to think that it is sometimes so easy! Whenever I got asked if I could help with something, I always immediately thought, "Of course I can!" because I didn't want to let the other person down. I thought that I could somehow make it work by taking away something of mine. But that wasn't working anymore, so beginning to say no was an important first step.

One night in the fall of 2015, we were sitting on the couch at home watching TV. It was a health show and they were saying that it is unhealthy for men to have a waistline over 37 inches. I was thinking I was fine, but I measured my waist and it was 41 inches. Wow, I did not see that coming. And then it was like all the bad things from the last few months came crashing over me. I didn't eat healthy food, I was tired all the time, and I needed an extra piece of chocolate to get me through the afternoon. I remembered driving one of the boys to handball practice and he was talking about healthy snacks. I knew what to eat but when he talked about how bad candy, cookies, and things like that are, I realized that was exactly the stuff I ate, so I knew I was eating the wrong stuff and yet I kept doing it. I also remembered when a guy at the gym started talking to me. He told me he had been on vacation and joked about how gluttony really was one of the seven deadly sins, and that he now had to suffer and really work out. And I thought, "Why did he start talking to me and why did he tell me that story?"

When I measured my waist after the TV show and saw that it was "too much," I remembered that car ride and that guy at the gym. That was three things reminding me about good health, and I felt the need to change; my body needed to be healthy. What could I do? I decided to quit added sugar—no more candy or cookies from then on. And I would start exercising three times a week; up until this point I exercised on a highly irregular basis. My first thought? "I wonder what Mom is going to say at Christmas; she always makes a lot of candy and cookies and cakes."

After my first gym session, I decided to stay and have a shower and a sauna. But then I felt bad. Should I really spend time in the sauna? Shouldn't I go home and do stuff? Surely there was something I should do rather than take that time for myself. I felt selfish for thinking about myself, but at the same time I had to listen to my body when it told me what I needed to feel good. Maybe there were others in that sauna thinking the same thing. Have you ever felt bad about making time for yourself?

The company I worked for had a winter party in January. I really didn't feel like going but I went anyway because "I'm supposed to." I spoke to a colleague about wanting to take some time off, and he said, "Take a leave of absence, they'll grant you that, you've done so much good." It felt nice to hear someone else say that I had done good things; it gave me power to listen more to myself and start taking the time I needed. I began to feel that I would find my place somehow. After that party I decided to scale down and avoid the company social events outside of working hours. Before, I had said yes to everything and participated fully, but now I couldn't do it; it didn't feel like fun and I needed a break.

As I have said before, I was always a social person and an active member in many different groups, and perhaps I was somewhat of a seeker, looking for meaning, trying to find my place in life. I looked for different groups where I would fit in, but never really gave it enough time and energy to actually end up feeling like I fit in. I almost always felt like an outsider. I sought out different contexts and situations, tried new things, and it worked well and people liked me. But I never fully trusted and accepted that I was liked. I created a barrier and kept people away, creating distance between us. I remember specifically one situation when I met some old university buddies. We had spent a lot of time together and about a year after we had all graduated and started our different careers, I got invited to a wedding. I declined; I was renovating an apartment and said that I didn't have time to go, but what I really thought was that they had only invited me out of sympathy. I have had that thought in many contexts: "We're only inviting Thomas because everyone else in the gang has been invited." Now I know that I was being too hard on myself.

It is difficult to pinpoint what caused this feeling in me. And I think that many people who know me don't understand it. They saw me as a person with a big social circle, a well-liked person, easygoing—and that was true. I was that person, I knew what to do, I had fun, I got to know lots of people, and I had many acquaintances. But I missed true closeness and openness. Did they really like *me*—or did they like the role I played?

CHAPTER 5

The Eye Opener

Saturday, February 13, 2016

We're now a ways into the new year—new challenges and new opportunities, as they say, but how does that relate to me? I've felt like I want to scale back. I haven't felt like dealing with anything new, just want to focus on what I have.

I felt it in the fall and talked to Lovisa, and she said that the only person who can put the brakes on is me. So, my goal is to focus on the clients and projects I already have, and yet this week there was more, and I couldn't say no. It's tricky. I have also begun to think that it would be fun to start my own business, it would be fun to try, to be the boss. I have a lot in my head and it hasn't settled yet, but I feel like I need a break, to get away, pause and reflect. It feels as if time is just slipping away, I do things for others, fix things around the house, walk the dog, drive the kids to games and practices, fix things at work, have a driving role, listen, fix, but I don't ever get the long break that I need. Sure, I can just take it, it just feels so strange, what I really want to do is to be alone, not having things that need to be fixed but just seeing what the day brings. Just had a feeling: sometimes I don't want to plan, decide, it depends on how I feel at the time and what the situation is at the time. I get stressed if something has to be decided about the future. But that's not always the case, I also like to plan trips and other things. I wonder what it is that makes me feel like that? Could it be that I promise something and then feel caged in and obliged to fulfil it and not disappoint people? I think there is a sense of duty there that makes me feel boxed in if I promise things... I'll have to get back to that.

C and I have had good conversations lately, we've cleared up a few things but it feels as if there's more before we're back to normal again. But we have different opinions about how things have been, she says I talk a lot and don't ask questions and I think that she has had so much to deal with and that I have chosen to keep away and focus on my things. And that she does so many things and when she's at home she has no energy left to do things with me and the kids. But it's good that we've begun to talk. And she is right about me talking a lot, because I've grown tired of not having any space. Although maybe I've mostly been talking about practical matters, we haven't talked to each other properly...

Yes, it feels as if a lot is happening inside me now. A feeling of taking up space, believing more in myself, being calmer when meeting new people. I mean, I'm good at meeting people, so what I'm talking about here is the ability to be myself on a deeper level and feel that it's okay that people like me for who I am. It's always there in the back of my head... But there's a time for everything, and what I feel like now is silence, serenity, and time for things to settle. I'm tired of socializing and always being up and about and feeling responsible for everyone else's wellbeing... That's why I don't want to be at the office but rather at a café—to escape having to talk about unnecessary things, just be myself, and I guess that's what I need right now and that's okay.

It's not the right time to try something new, instead I need to collect myself and recharge my batteries. Okay, so how do I recharge my batteries?

- *Exercise, change gyms, have a shower and a sauna afterwards*
- *Run*
- *Walk the dog by myself*
- *Be calmer in conversations, listen, ask questions, not take things as an attack*

- *Go away and be myself, follow the feeling*
- *Not just sit still at home with my phone and stuff but really rest.*

Yes, we'll try that and see where it takes me.

At this point I began to follow a feeling, an inner voice. I had an insight: things had not been good, and I needed to break patterns and habits to feel better. I had lost balance through a bad diet, and I hadn't been well. I didn't know what would happen but I had a strong feeling that I had to listen to what my body told me. And it told me to take care of myself, exercise and eat well, and to be calm. In the past, I "escaped" but I now chose to pause; I wanted to understand and change things for the better even if it was challenging and unfamiliar. I had the opportunity to attend Lovisa's yoga class eight Tuesdays in a row. Tried it once and thought that it was probably better if I ran or did more strenuous exercise instead, but then I got a feeling that told me to do yoga every week and I followed that feeling. And it was a good choice, because it brought me calm and allowed me to focus on reflecting and on my breathing.

Following my feelings and intuition is something I had done before, but at this time I had forgotten how to do it. Instead, I had soldiered on, focusing on all the musts and things I "should" do. I had lost a part of myself that used to exist naturally, and I had played many roles to fit in and please other people. To me, intuition is the thing that bubbles up in my mind, the feeling that I should head in a certain direction, it grows stronger and stronger—even if I don't know exactly what will come of it. A clear example of this is when I quit my job at Volvo. It was a very tough and risky thing to do, but I just felt that I had to do something else even if I didn't know exactly what that would be. Another clear example is the feeling I had when C and I got together; it involved many challenges—how would I handle having children, how would everything work out—but I just followed my feeling, which told me that this was the road I was supposed to take.

Many different authors and books have influenced me in that direction, to follow my feeling or intuition more. It started around 2009 as I began to absorb these new thoughts. I had just passed 30 and was in a transformational phase in life. I had recently ended my first long term relationship, things were changing at work, and I guess I had my first crisis about what to do with my life. At the same time, I attended a long leadership and personal development course at Volvo that really got me thinking.

One of the first books was *The Celestine Prophecy* (James Redfield, 1995), which a friend had told me about. My friend told me to read it after we had talked about feeling things intuitively. I talked about different things that I could usually feel, but that I didn't follow the feeling and that things often didn't work out the way I had hoped. I realized that I should have trusted in the feeling I had. I bought the book on a Friday and was immediately hooked, finishing it over the weekend. And that same weekend something happened that strongly influenced me and made me believe in and follow my feelings and intuition. As I said, I was completely immersed in the book and had read all through the Saturday. The book mainly takes places in Lima, Peru, and it speaks a lot about following your feelings and that things happen for a reason. At this time, I was single and had joined an online dating community. I had been a member for a couple of months and put in my profile that I was interested in women living in the Gothenburg region, and had also chatted with a few women in the area. During the time I had been a member, I had only connected with and received messages from women in and around Gothenburg. On that Sunday morning, I checked my email. And I had a message from a woman in Lima, Peru! I mean, what is the likelihood of that!? That the weekend I am reading that book I get a message from the city in which the book takes place? Believe what you want, to me this was a strong signal: you should continue in this direction, continue to listen to your feelings and follow that road.

Since then, I have read extensively from many different genres. I read all the sequels to *The Celestine Prophecy*. Took the wonderful books of Paulo Coelho to heart. Reflected upon Eckhart Tolle's books *The Power of*

Now and *A New Earth*, which are about living in the present. I also read the Swedish *Konsten att leva innerligt* ("The Art of Living Sincerely"), which presents Kierkegaard's different perspectives on doing more with your life. That book speaks beautifully about sensing something, that it is time for the next step, to leave something old to make room for something new and bigger. As an old engineer and a person who strongly believes in modern science, I didn't want to admit that I read such hippy dippy books—but I loved them! They gave me a fresh and beautiful perspective on life, on following my feelings, and thinking that people I meet are there for a reason. When you meet someone, you must have the courage to talk about whatever is on your mind, because that is the purpose of the encounter. I have had so much fun doing that, and it has given me so much more: my first job after Volvo, that I had the courage to meet C.

I have also had an interest in psychology, especially cognitive behavioral therapy and schema therapy, and I have read tons of books by many different authors. During my time at Volvo, I also had the benefit of attending many leadership courses which contained a lot of practical exercises that helped me grow as a person.

All this literature has had a huge influence on me, and together with the leadership courses it has given me the courage to try new things and be open to new perspectives on life. I have tried yoga, I have tried new alternative treatments, because why not? I have tried different treatments in which you follow energy flows through your body, for example craniosacral therapy. Another thing was Access Bars, a treatment based on releasing tensions in the body that come from old, unprocessed memories that get stuck in the body. I also took a leap and went on yoga retreats, where I was often, but not always, the only man. Believe me, as an old engineer and logical person, these were things I had not tried before. But all these things became pieces in puzzle, allowing me to be more and more open for different perspectives and opportunities. And I am very glad for this—otherwise I wouldn't be where I am today.

Unfortunately, I had forgotten many of these insights by early 2016, and I just kept going. I focused on my family, my work, how to make time for everything and what my role should be. It was all about what I should do, and I had forgotten myself and the things I needed. However, a small but still strong insight awoke here, telling me that my body and mind needed to feel better. I had to pause and take care of myself. That strong feeling gave me the power to change my diet, start exercising more, and pause for reflection.

Saturday, February 27, 2016

Sitting at a café in Malmö, took the train here to meet Ina, an old friend from my dancing days who runs a yoga center. Last spring, C and I were at a yoga retreat that Ina managed. Today we're going to talk about being a highly sensitive person. I was planning to come down here for a retreat but it didn't work out, so I went down this weekend instead and booked a private session with Ina. It's going to be exciting to see where it leads, we're getting together in 30 minutes, so I'm taking the opportunity to write a bit during lunch.

Ina is a friend whom I met for the first time in 2005 when we took the same class at a lindy hop camp in Herräng, the world's biggest lindy hop camp. I started dancing lindy hop in 2004, danced a lot and went to camps all over the world for many years. Ina and I had a lot of contact around 2010 as we were both in transformational phases with new insights, and we shared our thoughts about books we read and how they influenced us. We followed each other for a long time (and we still do), and I saw her develop, founding a yoga center in Malmö and then different yoga retreats. Ina is a friend whom I really trust and feel comfortable talking with about anything that is on my mind, even the hippy dippy stuff.

I caught up with Ina before Christmas and she said to me, "Thomas, you might be a highly sensitive person." That was an unfamiliar term, but I was interested in learning more about it. It fitted into the feeling I had and resonated with my thoughts, questions, and reflections about my recurring patterns. Ina had previously given me Access Bars treatments, so I thought, "Why not try this HSP thing too?" Even if I believed in it and wanted to try, it was a challenge to go all the way down to Malmö to talk more about it. I didn't tell my friends, I just said I was going down for a yoga thing. The fear of what others might think came back: "What a hippy dippy thing, you're an engineer, do you believe in that stuff…"

February 27, 2016, continued

I have now had three hours of treatment, and it was great but now that I'm writing about it I feel like I don't remember anything ☺ But I'll try to summarize. Many tensions were released and many tears, I must have courage to believe in who I am, help others where it's easy for me to do so, it's not about me being better than anyone else because it's easy for me, it's just something I'm good at. Being good at being me is not a bad thing. I choose to let go of limitations and do the things I'm good at, others can choose to do the same thing, but it's their choice and not mine… If others feel bad and want help, I can help—but it's their choice if they don't want any help, and they are adults and can make their own choices, it's not my responsibility. I'm bubbly with ideas and feel talkative, and that's okay, make it into a strength and be whatever feels easy to be.

With my family: Be more straightforward, be who I am, do things with the kids according to my ways, talk to the kids about how we have different perspectives on doing things our way and their dad's way. At work: Stand up for what I believe in. Be confident and stand up for my ideas, insecurity will shine through. In my groups (friends etc.): Continue as it is, have fun, it should be easy. Be grateful, accept thanks when given and give thanks when I should. Start my own business if I want to, follow my feelings and believe in my own greatness. That's all I can write now…

I will try to describe what happened that day. So many tensions in my body were released, so many old feelings resolved. It began with me talking about how I felt, what was on my mind and how I was doing. I talked about all the musts and things I should do, and Ina guided me through my emotions. A lot came up, especially things I have thought that I couldn't do but should. One simple thing that Ina said at the beginning was, "What if you are okay the way you are?" Such a simple thing, but I immediately thought, "What do you mean, okay the way I am?" I have to do stuff and fix things. But again, Ina said, "What if you are okay and your feelings and thoughts are okay?" It was a relief to be able to talk without being judged or worried about saying the wrong thing! I was in an environment that allowed me to be brave enough to be vulnerable. How often do we experience that? Are we brave enough to talk about our feelings or are we afraid to say the wrong thing and be excluded? Imagine the benefits of being in an environment that allows us to express our feelings and show our innermost selves. It was very important for me to slowly and somewhat incoherently put my emotions into words. By uttering the words, it was as if my thoughts materialized in the real world and I saw everything in a new light. It allowed me to move on, taking the first steps on a new journey where I wasn't trapped by my own emotions.

If I did more of the things that made me feel good, if I chose in my best interests and others didn't like it, it was their choice. I didn't always have to adapt and change my mind because somebody else thought differently. I realized that I must have more courage to listen to my feelings and work out what I need. If I always did things for other people and never for me, then how kind was I towards myself? If I neglected myself and only did things for others, I would burn myself out. And then I wouldn't be able to help others either. So, by choosing in my best interests and thereby having more energy, I can be there for others more often. It seems as if we tend to forget this today. We are supposed to do things for others because that makes us good people. But if we sacrifice ourselves, we also show others that it is not important to take care of ourselves. What do we teach our children if we always give up our own time? This was a new perspective for me, to choose what is good for me and thus have more energy to help others.

I talked to Ina about how I like to think and philosophize, view things from different perspectives, and how I think and feel things. But I have always thought that whatever I feel is not true or right, that there is something wrong with me. I have always had that basic idea that I am wrong. I have thought so through everything that has happened at home and at work, in everything that I have felt. I have thought that I am wrong, that I shouldn't make a fuss, that I am being ridiculous, that I have misinterpreted or misunderstood the situation. I have also avoided bringing things up for discussion because "I am wrong anyway." Even when discussing things and someone says something else, I have thought that I was wrong and backed down. It was such a relief to begin to realize that all the things I have felt and thought over the years have not been wrong. And I also asked myself the questions: How often do we do this, that we don't dare speak up because we convince ourselves that we are wrong? And how often do we choose not to listen to the other person?

Now that I have gained some perspective, I can see that it wasn't so strange that I shut off my emotions. According to research on highly sensitive persons, HSPs adapt very quickly to fit in. Both as infants and during childhood. I remember many situations during my childhood which I now see in a different light. Up until 6th grade, everything was quiet and harmonic at school; we played and had a lot of fun, and I felt good. But middle school and 9th grade was very tough. My mother told me that I was a sensitive kid and that a harsh word could make me cry. I was a good student, got good grades, and I remember how scared I was of being criticized by my teachers. What if I didn't know the answer or hadn't done my homework and I got the question, what would I say, of course I had to do my homework. What would happen if I didn't do it; then they might not like me anymore, I would make them disappointed.

As you can see, I was already stuck with demands on achievements, and unconsciously I felt that the things I achieved, the things I did—that was who I was. Thus, if I failed at something I did, it felt as if *I* was a failure. But that is not true, and I believe that many people today struggle with similar problems. So, imagine if we could see ourselves and each other more for who we are than for what we do. And if we, at an early age, can learn to understand emotions as a key to understanding ourselves.

I also remember being good at math, and as I finished the 6th grade math book early, I was asked if I wanted to start on the 7th grade math book. But I didn't, because what would happen then—I was already the nerd who stood out. As I said, middle school was tough because the quiet and safe environment of elementary school was gone. The 9th graders immediately picked on us 7th graders and found the ones they could mess with. I don't think I ever thought I was being bullied, and I probably wasn't, but it was tough. I felt that I stood out; I was tall and grew a moustache early, but I didn't want to shave because that would make me an adult and I was only 13 years old. Things were good in my class though, and I was the one that everyone talked to, especially the girls. But the older students picked on me and I felt that I had to avoid certain things. So, I became careful not to stand out.

One thing that was on my mind when I wrote this diary entry is the fact that while things were tough, I was doing well at school; my grades were good, I played handball, had good teammates, played the saxophone. I was a person who fixed things and did well for myself. Lots of kids came to me for help, but I would never ask for any help myself or talk about what was on my mind. Among the boys, it was mostly joking and fighting, and to be openly insecure and talk about feelings or thoughts was not right. It was important to fit into the macho environment and you were afraid of being called names if you broke the norm. I remember one time; it was a vote for the school Lucia[3] and someone

---

3   On the 13th of December, children in Sweden dress up as Saint Lucy, and as star singers and elves. In each school, one girl is chosen to be Saint Lucy, or Lucia, herself

had put a picture of me in the jar. I remember how tough that was to go through, but of course I didn't tell anyone how I felt about it. I also remember how I felt when I got good grades in 9th grade; 4.7 out of 5 in the old grade system. I hardly dared to tell anyone about it and I almost apologized for having such good grades, because it was a part of the macho norm to not be good at school. I got good grades in high school too, but I didn't want to work too hard because I didn't want my grades to look too good.

So many feelings bubbled up during the session with Ina, and we talked about how all the feelings I have felt were okay. Things that happened a long time ago and the feelings I carried with me—they were okay. The defense I constructed in my teens—I didn't need it anymore. I could see what I have done and felt, and it made me sad that I have limited my life and that I felt the way I did. I began to understand, and the pieces of the puzzle fell into place. I realized that I haven't been aware of it, but I have picked up on other people's discomfort, dislike, or anger, and I have unconsciously adapted to it. It is a part of our upbringing that we learn what to do and how to behave to not stand out or be "wrong"—both with peers and teachers. We sense what is expected and we do things to avoid problems and please others. Childhood, and especially the teenage years, is a sensitive period, and to keep your own needs to yourself when you really need to express your thoughts and ideas is very limiting if you are a sensitive and contemplative soul.

I believe that I shut off a lot during middle school. I didn't want to stand out, so I didn't dare talk about my thoughts with my friends, because what if they exposed me for all the others. And to talk with my teachers or parents about my problems—what would happen then, they thought that everything was going so well, and I was doing so well at school. Both my mom and my dad said, "There are no problems with Thomas. He's happy and kind and doing well at school." I probably didn't

---

and wears a crown with candles on it and leads the procession. Songs are sung and special saffron buns are baked.

reflect on it at the time, but now I can see that a highly sensitive person like me obviously picked up on the situation and didn't want to bother them by telling them that the situation was anything other than what they imagined.

When I talk and am being social as an adult, I remember different situations, and I feel the differences in my body. I think being a lecturer and a teacher is fun; I appreciate questions and like to contribute with my knowledge. I like to be a project manager, driving things forward, making sure the group is doing well, listening and sensing and making sure that everyone's voice is heard. And it also feels good when I talk to people one on one. But when I am in a group, like when grabbing coffee or with friends at a restaurant, it's difficult. I worry that what I am saying is not interesting or fun, and what if they think I am boring when I talk to them. I begin to talk faster so that I won't take up too much space, and I also talk more quietly, making it difficult to hear what I say—which means that the group doesn't hear me. Thus, my fear is realized; what I say is not interesting because I don't believe in myself, and they can't hear me because I talk too fast and too quietly.

As I mentioned, it was a huge relief to hear that my thoughts and emotions are okay. To just be allowed to talk about all the things I have kept inside. To hear that it was okay to be good at school. That it is okay to continue to do the things I think are fun and the things I am good at. That it is okay to listen to my feelings. That it is okay to balance a lot of things simultaneously, that I think about what to say instead of answering questions immediately. It was also a big thing to be helped and allowed to cry when all the difficult emotions bubbled up. Several times, I apologized for crying, for letting myself feel. Sometimes I held the tears back, but Ina made sure I let them out and allowed myself to cry. And by crying, so much was resolved. But what about men who cry? What have I been told since childhood? Men don't cry, men are strong and don't show emotions. But is that true? Or is it, in fact, by having enough courage to show your emotions and be vulnerable, that you are strong and true to yourself?

It was also a relief to talk about and understand how I take responsibility for other people. How I try to solve other people's problems and how it takes away a lot of my energy. And Ina said, "What if you are not responsible for other people, what if they are grown-up enough to make their own decisions?" That really hit me. I tried to help others when I thought they needed to feel better; I took on the responsibility of solving their problems. I know I can help by listening and being supportive, but I shouldn't take the responsibility—it is not mine to take. Sometimes I haven't even been asked to solve someone else's problem, I have just taken over it. This was an eye opener. I want to be kind and helpful, but by taking over the responsibility I show that I don't trust the other person to be a grown-up capable of solving her or his own problems. Instead of helping them, I do them a disservice.

Another thing Ina said was, "Other people make their own choices; what you can do is to tell them how their choices affect you. Then you get to decide how you want to act based on that." If someone chooses to do something that I don't like, then I can tell them how I feel about it. And if they don't want to change their mind, I can choose to leave.

Sunday, February 28, 2016

Today is a quiet day. I have slept really well, went to the hotel gym before breakfast, then had a good breakfast, read a bit, and went for a walk. I'm now relaxing at a café.

I'm feeling very calm and harmonic, my mind is calm, nothing that I need to get off my chest in writing, like yesterday. Instead, I feel good and I'm relaxed. It's the kind of feeling I've been searching for, but I haven't understood what it means. Now, I need to keep this feeling, I will continue to believe in myself, do the easy things, make my own choices and believe in them. If I become a manager and/or start my own business, I'm not better than anyone else. I make my choices and everyone else makes theirs and different people find different things easy. The fact that I'm good at what

I do and want to be even better does not make me a better person than other people. I choose to develop in areas I'm good at, and that is a choice we can all make.

And I cannot make choices for other people. I can have opinions and I can help them, but if they don't want my help, it's their choice and I need to be clear about what feels good for me.

I will believe in myself and what I do, I will not yield but remain who I am. I will not let anyone else step on me or give in if something doesn't feel good. In that case, I'll give it time, try to get some air and understand why it's needed.

I will be there for my friends and family, be more open and follow my feelings straight away. I will talk with the kids, make sure that they are allowed to be sensitive and that they understand that we all see things differently.

I'm a highly sensitive person and proud of it. It has been tough, but I now understand what it means. Many things bubble up in me, my thoughts are jumping around, I want to "play" and not be so serious, make sure that things are more relaxed, and have fun. Now I know that I can be myself, I don't have to be nervous about how other people view me. If I'm calm and believe in myself, have confidence, things are so much better; if I'm insecure then others will sense it and it becomes a vicious circle.

The new time has begun ☺

CHAPTER 6

New Habits

Thursday, April 7, 2016

Woke up early today, at 5 am, and it's now 5:45. Yesterday I woke up even earlier, at 4 and lay in bed thinking. It feels as if things are moving up and down right now, met the manager yesterday at the company where I hoped that I might start working, the door is not closed but I had hoped things would move faster. Then I had to deal with some stuff with my sales manager, he never finishes and keeps avoiding the question, I get so tired and it bugs me. The worst part is that it invades my thoughts, I woke up annoyed now wondering how I should reply to the email from my sales manager. So how does it get any better than this? ☺ Read some of what I wrote last time, what a difference.

What made my irritation and disappointment from yesterday go away was the "be brave" that C sent me yesterday. I realize that it can be difficult to do, to be exposed, bare yourself, be brave enough to ask without knowing how it will turn out and think about failed expectations and hopes. But dreaming, envisioning, and daring to hope is something I want to do. Because if I don't dare, I will stand still, it is all about having courage and lots of ideas, and something good will happen. I mustn't put all my expectations in one area.

So, what do I do now? Well, I'll continue with my ideas, go for whatever feels easy—have fun, dare!!! Have vision, share ideas, show my point of

*view—and I can't make choices for other people, just show them my per-
spective. I mustn't be disappointed over their choices because they're theirs
and not mine. I can only do my best and be my best self. And have fun!* ☺

Now that spring was here, there were a few things that I took with me
and tried to implement: making more decisions and choices for me,
feeling what it was I needed, and doing my job while respecting myself.
I began to put me-time into the work calendar to have enough time for
planning, and "space" for unexpected things. It was a simple thing to do
but very important, because if there was even a small hole in the calendar, someone would book a meeting. It was vital that I could find and
control my own time if I was going to be able to do a good job. If possible,
I worked somewhere other than the office; sometimes I began the day at
a café if I was just emailing or putting together a presentation. It felt good
to spend time in another setting and not be constantly interrupted with
questions. By asking myself the simple questions (such as, "What do I
need to make my day work?" and "What do I need to do a good job?"),
I began to create a situation that suited me better, and my employer was
okay with it too. I began to take responsibility for my work situation and
have courage to say what I needed. Of course, it depended on how I felt
on a given day, and on what kind of assignment I had, but by raising the
question, things started to get better.

It takes time for changes to manifest in the body. My insights from
February had to settle and everything was not going to change overnight.
But I began to be conscious about it and step by step I started to follow
my feelings. Gradually, I also took new initiatives, and it felt good to have
support from different people. But it was also a challenge to do things
differently. It felt unfamiliar, both to me and to the people around me,
when I began to change my behavior. There was a different dialogue at
work, and I stopped accepting some things that I accepted before. Naturally, there was some friction, and I realized that I must give it time; these
were habitual behaviors that had existed for a long time. At the same

time, there was a kind of expectation from others that I should behave a certain way. It helped to think about how I would react if someone else changed their behavior, if someone did something one way yesterday and said no today. How long would it take for me to get used to the new way? Thinking like this makes you respect that things must be allowed to take time to settle, in others and in yourself.

Tuesday, May 10, 2016

Nice summer heat since Thursday. It was over 20° Celsius this weekend and it's stayed hot. I'm sitting in our new "sun corner," with the sofas that we bought. We've cleaned the flagstones in the patio, bought new outdoor furniture, a corner sofa, a corner table and an armchair, then a new table and eight outdoor chairs. It looks great, like the boys said, "We have an-other room." Feels great ☺ I've missed this, last summer we didn't spend that much time outdoors, I didn't like it and wanted to have more of it and now it's ready. So I hope it'll be a great summer!

A lot has happened since last I wrote, with work and my confidence. It's been a lot with clients, leadership positions at my company and meeting people about a new job opportunity, and I have been up and down, wanting to quit and really disliking my position. But it has brought something good with it. I have had more courage to speak my mind at work, to my manager, the regional manager and others, and with good results. I think I have been worried that it has all been in my head, but I now have a feeling that I can believe more in what I think and feel, in front of my managers and people with power as well. Speaking up has relieved the heavy feeling at work. I go for what I believe in and have the courage to speak more instead of being angry and saying nothing… Then I had a couple of bad meetings about the new job opportunity—a meeting with the CEO made me back away and actually say no to the job. It felt good, however, and it brought some positive things as they took the feedback to heart and we now have a new dialogue. We'll get in touch again after the summer, so we'll see what happens there.

I also said no to being a part-time group manager at my company. Perhaps it was a little odd to say no to an opportunity like that, but I feel that I need to think about what I really want to do and aim higher. Not just accept what others want me to do or think I can handle. Of course I can do it, but is it really what I want? All of this has made me stronger; I believe more in myself, in what I can do, I take more space and believe in my capability. I haven't set all my goals yet, but it feels good to do what I do now, I'm doing a good job and it's working out well. I don't need that gnawing worry about not being good enough. Believe in what I do, focus on what I do, and don't say yes to everything just to please others. I need to be pleased first, then I can help others because I will have more energy.

One positive contributor is my increase in exercise. I have lost 10 kg. Been to good yoga classes with Lovisa, which have given me a calm and techniques to use at home. C also likes her job; she started February 1st, so it's been a lot this spring. In a good way ☺ Now I'm going to relax, enjoy the good feeling, focus on what I do and have the courage to stick my neck out. I will take on new challenges with high spirits and think about what the next step will be.

Thanks to exercise, yoga, and a change in the way I worked, I made time for relaxation and recovery. The exercise gave me time for reflection, things were allowed to settle, and my body felt better. It was absolutely a challenge to change my routines and start exercising more. But at the same time, I knew that I needed it and I knew that doing something different feels uncomfortable for a while before it becomes a habit. It was good to remind myself of the feeling that comes after working out—it was hard at first but afterwards I was really happy with myself. I chose to do yoga once a week for two months. It was a good choice and it gave me a lot. It helped my thoughts to settle, and I took simple yoga and breathing exercises with me to use at home. Simplicity became an important concept for me, and it was also very important to find those moments where I could do yoga or breathing exercises. You don't have to be away for two hours—as long as you have 15–20 minutes, you can do a couple of simple exercises.

It was also a real challenge at first to change my diet and stop eating foods with added sugar. One thing that kept coming back during the first stages of my transformation was how other people would react and think. It was close to Christmas and I remember the time I had to tell my mom about my new diet. Imagine coming home for Christmas and not eating any of the candy or cookies. My mom understood me, of course, and I think that all of my family members now eat less sweets. One thing that helped me break the habit was a kind of mantra I used. I have chosen to not eat sugar, it is my choice; I can eat it if I want to—but I don't want to. That thought—"I can eat as much as I want, but I don't want any"—really made it easier for me. Another thing I noticed when I stopped eating added sugar was that I started eating better in general. For example, I avoided heavy lunches in favor of lighter meals. Prior to this, I often experienced low blood sugar and became irritable and grumpy. I had to watch my temper, especially in the evenings before dinner. I noticed a big difference there; my temper was much more even, and I didn't experience the same low blood sugar. If I didn't eat, I might get a bit tired, but it didn't affect my mood in the same way. Earlier when I had low blood sugar, I had to eat right away, and it wasn't always the healthiest food. Now, I was calmer and made more conscious and healthy choices when it came to eating.

Thanks to my recovery, I also began to listen to my feelings more. I was stronger, trusted my feelings, and had the courage to speak my mind to others. For a long time, I could sense a bad mood at work, but thought that it was just me. However, I now began to think that perhaps it wasn't all me. I started checking in with colleagues, and they agreed about the bad mood. Their stories supported my own view of people being tired, worn out and that they felt pressure to deliver more and more. Several of the people I spoke with had been burned out or been on part-time sick leave due to burnout. It meant a lot to me to check if my feeling was correct by asking my colleagues. It gave me the courage to speak up; I wasn't alone, and I was very happy that I raised these questions. Eventually, I spoke with my manager and the regional manager, we had a meeting and I told them about what I had discovered and the mood at work. They took it well and were glad that I had raised the matter for discussion. Their reception was a great confirmation.

At work, I continued to follow my feelings and say no to more and more of the voluntary evening activities. They were often fun, and I had attended before, but at this time I needed quiet and continued recovery. I also had the courage to say no to a company trip in August. Before, I always felt that I was being boring if I said no to that kind of thing, and that I should take part in all activities. However, I was now better at sensing what I needed—and at this time, I didn't have the energy to participate, and that was okay. And of course, there were no weird reactions from my colleagues or managers; nobody said anything other than that it was okay for me to stay at home.

Another thing that showed that I was recovering from my burnout is that I now had the energy to do things around the house. The year before, I couldn't do anything about the patio. For a person who is burned out, even small things can seem like insurmountable obstacles. And it was really the case for me; small things that "should" take five minutes to do were very difficult. I felt accused, had no me-time but "had to" do a lot of stuff. But now, when my energy was replenished, I fixed up the patio and everything around it easily. Today, when I look back at it with the perspective I now have, it seems so easy, but when you are in the middle of a burnout and are a person who wants to fix things, your body tenses up. It was also difficult for the people around me who had a constantly tired person around who didn't have the energy to do anything but at the same time wouldn't let anyone else do those things. It was a challenge for everyone involved.

Wednesday, June 15, 2016

Wednesday evening, relaxing at home. C is out having coffee with some guy and I'm thinking about life. It feels like I'm taking steps forward when it comes to trusting my feelings and beliefs. It was tough tonight when C left to have coffee with a guy she finds interesting. It's okay for me but it's still tough—perhaps because we're going through a rough patch. I just called Daniel and talked with him for a while, and it was good to talk to him about C and work. It's important to talk about the heavy stuff, the stuff that's on my mind—and feel that it's okay. I feel that I limit myself and that it's time to let go of certain things. Be brave enough to let go and open up for something new. Let go of clients and projects at work and do something new. Leave the people I've worked with for years and find that new thing.

Have the courage to talk with C, discuss the important things and not beat around the bush. I feel that I limit myself in the things I say because there's history there, should I have done this or that, stuff that I should be thinking about, but it becomes an obstacle. I shouldn't have to adapt all the time, I am who I am, and if I'm not interesting then perhaps we shouldn't continue to be together. If I'm not perfect, be happy with who I am and that I mean well. So, it's time to speak up and speak from the heart. Not always do as I'm told but instead do what feels good and be willing to meet disagreement. If we're splitting up, it's better to do it now than letting time slip away.

It feels a bit strange to write this and perhaps it is… ☺ But the sense of joy and happiness must be expressed, and I express it by being honest with myself, being willing to disagree, and having the courage. But I won't say everything that's on my mind—I'll do it in a smart way. Stop brooding, talk and act instead. That goes for work too, if I feel like taking time off or doing something new, then I should do whatever feels easy and right and not care so much about what other people think. If I'm happy and deliver what I promise, then it's okay and good enough.

So many little things came up, things that might seem insignificant but were annoying. For example: for a long time, I was the one who made breakfast porridge for everyone each morning. Now, I didn't feel like it anymore, I wanted us to do it together now that the kids were older and could help. So, on the one hand I got grumpy because I had to do this for everybody, while on the other hand I didn't want to discuss it because I didn't want to be difficult. It really wasn't a big deal to make porridge, so I didn't say anything; I continued to make it, but I was a bit annoyed…

Here, I can see that I took a role based on how I "should" be, and I couldn't get out of it. I had an image of how I should behave in a relationship; I should fix a whole lot and not be difficult by fussing over little things. I think many people can identify with this, and that many of us get stuck in similar roles after we spend some time in a relationship. It is not strange at all that we change and evolve, and yet there are expectations about how we should behave and that we should stay the way we have always been. I started thinking things like, "If I make a fuss about little things, will she stop loving me?" I was also not used to dealing with disagreements and speaking my mind, because I hadn't practiced it. I confused the matter at hand with the relationship more broadly. I felt inadequate and wondered if it was just me being inexperienced.

It is interesting to note that I didn't have any problems dealing with disagreements at work or among friends; it was only in close relationships that disagreements became a challenge. Perhaps the consequences of a disagreement in a close relationship are more frightening than those of a disagreement at work, I don't know. As with other things, disagreement can awaken childhood memories (perhaps more so for a highly sensitive person). When stressed, you act in a way that you did when you were a child, and you do things that worked and were needed then, even if it is not a reaction you need as an adult. For me, it had to do with both my father and my brother being very quick to emotional reactions. They reacted quickly when something went wrong; for example, I remember how my father threw his slipper at the TV when the horses didn't run according to his bet, and how my brother quickly lost his temper when he lost at games. They were quick to emotional responses in arguments as well. My experience was that we went in separate directions and said, "Let's just drop it." My father simply walked away, grew silent and could sulk for days. And it was best to avoid my brother completely; you couldn't talk to him when he was angry. Thus, we never really had any discussions; my father and brother became angry and we never practiced having a dialogue or solving disagreements. And so, it was easier for me as an adult to not deal with conflict in a close relationship; instead, I walked away with unprocessed feelings.

In my experience, many of us are unaccustomed to talking about these little things because we don't want to be difficult. The risk is that someone will be angry or grumpy, or that the situation will become worse. I think that many people can identify with this. But the problem remains, there is a weird mood but we still don't talk about the elephant in the room. That is, we have an unresolved disagreement between us and it stays right there, even if we pretend it doesn't. And by not addressing it, we risk becoming annoyed, angry, miserable—these are little things, but they can grow into monstrous elephants.

We must have courage. We must be a little difficult. We must understand that we have different opinions and thereby admit that we have a disagreement. I talked to a friend from Italy who described the word 'conflict' in an interesting way. Being in conflict is called *confliggere* in Italian. If we break down the word, CON means 'together' and AFFLIG-ERE means "to give oneself pain, suffering, or worries" (compare it to the word 'afflict'). Being in conflict can thus be seen as a common or shared pain or anxiety that can only be resolved together. That is, both parties are suffering as long as you avoid the argument, and if you don't deal with it, it will remain unresolved.

If we defuse a disagreement and instead view it as two different experiences of the same situation, what happens then? There is no right or wrong, just different perspectives on a situation. You must also be able to separate the matter at hand from the relationship. I am an emotional person and separating those two have been difficult for me, which has led to my taking disagreement as attacks on my person. This has kept us from resolving the actual issue. But it is also easy to actually resort to personal attacks and talk about things that have happened in the past or how someone behaves, i.e. you enter into a relationship drama. That becomes counterproductive if you want to resolve the matter at hand. It can be difficult, but it is better to try and keep it simple and focus on the fact that there is a problem, an issue, that makes both parties suffer—and how do we resolve that issue? Entering into the argument then becomes a matter of clarifying, of seeing the other person's perspective, showing your own perspective, listening to each other, and then work it out together. And to be clear: resolving a disagreement is not about winning or losing, or of being right or wrong. It is about recognizing each other's perspectives and being more understanding of each other.

Thus, it doesn't help to keep a lid on it; it is important to talk about even the little things and the feelings that these things create, and about how you view different situations. And it has to be okay to change your mind—even if you have done one thing for a long time, made porridge for example, you must be allowed to grow tired of it and bring it up for discussion. It is important to practice talking about the little things, having the courage to bring them to light and not judge anyone. Imagine if you could play around with it and see it as practice. For example, you could say, "This might sound ridiculous, but one thing that's been on my mind for a long time is…" or "We haven't talked about this for a while, and you might think it's a small thing, but it bugs me…" It is very important to be open and not accuse the other person but just view the situation as it is. What should we do now? How can we change this? The keyword here is *we*.

Monday, July 25, 2016

Two weeks into the vacation, sitting on our comfy lounge sofa, it's around 7 pm, C is at the dog run and I'm relaxing at home. We spent the first week of our vacation in Dalarna, Monday to Friday. Great days, mixed weather and we went swimming between the rain showers, sometimes wearing our raincoats as we stepped into the water. It was fun to have the boys with us and it felt like everyone was happy. I know that things can be a bit tense at my dad's, but it's getting better and better, and I deal with it better too. My dad makes his own choices and I can't influence him, he is responsible for his own actions and I don't have to control and plan all the time.

I really needed this vacation, been feeling worn out for a while now, got through the last couple of weeks on willpower alone. Don't know what will happen now or how I feel about work and starting my own business. I won't think too much on it now, just relax, rest, and then follow my feelings. We'll see what happens. All for now!

CHAPTER 7

The Importance of Breaking Down

Österlen, Thursday, August 25, 2016

Today I woke up in Österlen[4], came down yesterday afternoon and will stay here for a yoga retreat Wednesday to Sunday. C and I were here two years ago and an old friend of mine, Ina, is one of the instructors.

What a morning! I woke up before the wake-up call, have taken a shower and now, at 7, I'm sitting on a bench enjoying the sunrise. I see a large field and the ocean, a wonderful view. It's already hot and it's going to be around 26 degrees Celsius today. The theme for this retreat is HSP step 2, I have been to Ina before and learned step 1 even if I didn't attend the retreat that time. It's going to be an exciting weekend, especially going into more depth about sensitivity. I've learned that I'm a highly sensitive person and accept it on a different level now. I dress myself in other people's emotions and I sense the mood very quickly, and this has affected me more than I think.

Yesterday when we began, and on the trip down here, I felt something bubbling in me, almost like I'm about to break down, and I almost started crying right away when it was my turn to talk. It was an odd sensation and I probably sensed the other people in the room, but it still feels as if something will rise to the surface in the next couple of days.

---

4   Österlen is a very picturesque region in southeast Sweden, part of the province of Skåne.

Yesterday evening when all of us gathered to share, I immediately recognized myself in their stories about being called sensitive, being affected by a group of people, absorbing a lot of stimulus. I now think it strange, I mean, it has always been easy for me to be in a group, to commit, talk to people, but I now feel more and more that I need me-time. Why is that? Is it because it's difficult to relax and find me-time? Yes, that is part of the answer, but also that I often take the role as helper, I fix things, get things done, help the new settle in. But I often like the start-up process, and then when it's more management and the same procedures every day, I don't like it anymore.

But what I realize will be difficult, or easy ☺, to talk about is my feelings of not fitting in. I always feel a little like an outsider in a group, and if I'm 100 % myself then everybody thinks I'm weird. That's why I play those roles—to fit in. I sometimes think that people are only being nice to me and that they don't actually want to spend time with me. Wow, it's very emotional to write about this.

Now I think it's time to start the day, I haven't heard any bell but I'll go check. I'll be back...

It was so great to hear the others tell their stories and be able to identify with their words. There were twelve other people and they all shared their stories, making me feel that I could share too. I already felt on the way down that something would happen; it felt as if I began to let go of a lot of old stuff that I had kept inside for many, many years. When I look back on my childhood, I remember experiencing that I thought and felt in a way that other people didn't. For example, I remember how I would make a contribution to a group discussion, but the group immediately went on to talk about something else. Was it because they didn't like what I said, because they thought my contribution was weird, or because they were just really into "their" subject right then? This made me unwilling to talk about certain subjects, especially how I felt. I realized that I wasn't alone with these thoughts, but it was difficult to talk about it at the time. How many of us are afraid to talk about things because we are afraid to stand out? Especially in our teens. That is what we do in childhood; we watch, learn, and adapt our behavior to fit in and stay in the group. I adapted and acted in a certain way to fit in. I avoided certain issues and thoughts because other people would laugh at them, joke about them, or ignore them. Or because they would make fun of me if I said it. These were small events, perhaps insignificant to others, but to me it closed doors and changed my behavior. We all take criticism differently and some are more sensitive about it than others. I remember being seen as a sensitive person, and I absorbed criticism very quickly.

It was also very important for me to "please" others; I didn't want to bother them with my problems. It wasn't always big things, but the small thoughts and doubts that come with growing up. I wonder if I fit in? What did they think of what I said? I wonder if that girl likes me? I didn't have the courage to be exposed and show people that I had questions too. Eventually, I buried these emotions and thoughts. And naturally, I didn't talk to anyone about it. Because I was different and my thoughts were wrong—at least, that is how I felt. What would happen if I brought these trifles up for discussion? It would only get worse. Better to keep quiet. And I always received positive words about being good at school, always behaving well, and that everything went so well for me. So why make a fuss?

I wonder how many of us share such thoughts. That we don't have the courage to be laid bare. How much baggage in the form of memories from our childhood or teenage years do we carry with us today, letting it limit us? Do we have that friend that we can trust and tell how we truly feel? Hearing the others at the retreat tell their stories gave me the courage to be vulnerable and share my thoughts. And I knew that these thoughts are only my image and experience of the world. I believe that it often has to do with our own fear of exposure, the fear of letting others see our vulnerability. That "truth"—that we are so different—is in our heads, I think. Don't you all have these thoughts and doubts that I have? And if all of us share these feelings and thoughts, why don't we talk about them more often?

Day 2 Österlen, Friday, August 26, 2016

Sitting on the same bench as yesterday, it's 6:30 and I woke up before the wake-up call again, feels great! This morning we're going down to the beach for morning yoga. It's a little windy now so we'll see what it's like by the sea.

Yesterday was an emotional day, we talked a lot about right and wrong and that there are no such things, instead it's all about being conscious of what feels light and what feels heavy. I have often thought about doing right, and that if a decision has been made it can't be changed. We talked about what stops us and what we make significant, and I brought up the whole "feeling like I don't fit in" thing. Wow, it's so much easier to write about it today ☺ I got some guidance and we talked about how I can let go of my fear of not fitting in, the fear of being lonely and being left out. How I can get close to other people by being more of myself. I spoke with another participant about this thing with the kids, that I feel like they're happy when I leave and happy when I'm not around. I mean, it's okay if I'm around but they are happier when I'm not and they can be alone with C. The participant I spoke to also had stepchildren and understood how I felt. She was very kind and realized that I was close to tears, and she said, "You look like you need a hug" and then I started to cry... It was good to talk about it, and this was before the guidance session, when even more emotions bubbled up. It's very liberating to cry and let go sometimes. And it was very interesting to listen to all the others and realize that I again could identify with their stories—very liberating.

Then we had a four-hour break, so I went to the beach, it was absolutely beautiful, then I went back here for a run. In the evening, we talked more about feelings and how they are energies that are neither positive nor negative, they are just energies. You should let the feeling pass, it's just energy that should be released, and it only takes a few minutes. We talked about the emotional curve, it's like a wave and you just have to let it roll. And if you resist the feeling, it will remain. What you resist persists. That feels like something I can take to heart, letting the feelings pass and be released. They are just energy.

I had planned to describe my guidance session in detail, but I realize that the best description is to say that I brought up the difficult stuff and let it go, I went to the core of the emotion and released it. There is a risk that it will come back, it's a familiar feeling. But I will tear down the wall and take in the positive instead, think about my friends and that they like me for who I am ☺

To be able to talk about my feelings of not being liked, that the kids secretly didn't like me; to talk about these things that I had kept inside for so long, to let it out and allow myself to be sad—it was such an incredible relief and so liberating. One of the best things about these discussions was the emotionally safe environment. We let everybody finish, nobody judged or gave answers to how one should feel or how a situation should be resolved. Our leaders worked with questions and got us to see things from new perspectives. We were allowed to start from where we were at that moment and take our own steps to understanding and insight. It was our own process and the steps we needed to take ourselves. As a listener in such situations, it might seem easy to see what the person should do, because you have been through it yourself and you know which steps the person need to take, and you want to be helpful and say it. But you have to think back to how it was for you, how you gained your own insights and did what you needed to do, and allow the speaker to do the same. The most important thing is that you get to do it at your own pace and that the people around are respectful of this. That is why the emotionally safe environment is so important.

The first time I talked about things like that, I felt that I was incoherent, because I hadn't talked about it before. I didn't have any expectations about people providing answers or a solution. I think that Brené Brown, who researches vulnerability, describes it well in her book *Rising Strong*. In this phase, you make a first draft, you begin to put your emotions and thoughts into words. These are the first words that pop up in your head, and they are most likely not the end result of your process. But to actually start talking and expressing yourself is important; the first draft is necessary. To expect a perfect result right away can even keep you from starting to talk at all. To me, it was the questions and the emotionally safe environment that opened up everything, and I could then work on perfecting my "draft." If we could all just listen, ask questions, and simply be there, I think more people would find the courage to talk about difficult things and eventually feel better. How would you like it to be and what do you need to talk more about?

It was also interesting to reflect on and talk about judging, about how feelings and thoughts cannot be right or wrong, about all these things we carry with us, and how we judge ourselves. I have often judged myself when I have made an error or mistake of some kind. What if I had said this or that instead? What if I had done that five years ago, what would it be like today? Why did I say that, I'm so stupid and clumsy... I realized that I still judged myself for a lot of things I should or shouldn't have done. All that was still in my head. But what if there is no right or wrong in how you think and feel? What if you don't have to judge yourself?

Naturally, we carry things with us so that we can learn how to act and function in society and develop as people. But to continue brooding about old mistakes leads nowhere; you get stuck. The important thing is that we get better at letting go of the thought of whether or not our action was the right one, and instead learn from the situation and look ahead. A first step is to think about what we carry with us in our emotional backpacks. It can be things that happened a long time ago but still limit us today, things that keep us from doing what we fear, things that we protect ourselves from even though they present no danger today. In my experience, we can have behaviors that helped us or were needed in certain situations but today they limit us because the situations are not the same. For example, you may have developed a certain behavior in your family, with old friends, or perhaps at school to protect yourself from bullies, and you retain that behavior at work or elsewhere even though the situation is different and may not be threatening.

We must allow ourselves to experience our feelings and let them pass, because what we resist will persist. Let the wave pass, don't try to hold it back. It is vital to understand how you react when a feeling comes and what your patterns are in order to allow and manage the feeling. It is also important to realize that it can be good to cry. To feel how the tension in your body relaxes, that things get easier afterwards. It was so great, the way that everyone in our group allowed each other to feel and show these feelings, and it was a contrast to how things usually are. In my experience, we have stopped allowing feelings, saying that it is wrong to let them out: "You shouldn't cry!" What if we instead could say, "Good, cry as much as you need, it's good to let your feelings out." Then you could ask, "What was it that made you sad?" How hard it can be to let yourself cry! You apologize for crying, like there is something wrong with it. But what if it is just a passing manifestation of your feeling? It is interesting to note the contrast between anger and sadness here. If a person (primarily a man, because this has a lot to do with norms) angrily runs off and slams the door behind him, then you might hear something like, "Oops, he got a bit angry, but it'll pass." If the person were to cry, however, you would probably instead hear something like, "Wow, he seems like a sensitive person, we have to be careful around him."

Which feelings are really okay in our society? That boys learn at an early age that anger is the only manifestation of feelings that is okay contributes to much frustration and dammed-up needs. We live in a society that in part is based on dammed-up feelings. In my experience, we have a kind of inheritance, especially we men; we are supposed to soldier on and take care of ourselves. We mustn't share our feelings, thoughts, and doubts. This inheritance keeps us from getting to know ourselves, from knowing how to deal with the ups and downs of life and understanding that feelings and thoughts are natural and that they will pass. But this inheritance can be cast off by you, if you can increase your own awareness. It is all about having the courage to be vulnerable, letting others be vulnerable, and creating a more emotionally safe environment.

By doing this, you will create an inner strength that allows you to master your emotions, and you can then be comfortable with yourself and support others on their journey to inner understanding. You don't have to pass on a destructive attitude to your children or the people around you. Social problems like violence and criminality, an unequal society, macho culture, homophobia—I think that much of it would decrease drastically if all of us, especially boys, were allowed to show feelings and be vulnerable, and if we all got better at understanding our emotional patterns and at talking about how we feel, without judging. What positive effects do you see? The change starts with you.

Day 2 Österlen, Friday, August 26, 2016, continued

It's around 5 pm, we went for a swim in the pool this afternoon. I also played a little saxophone in the garden, it was liberating to play outdoors knowing that other people could hear me, as it's something I've been afraid of. But I'm tearing down the wall and I feel safer with the saxophone, especially the thing that Marcus taught me about jazz scales, good stuff and it's easy to just play, it sounds great and it's good to play around with the notes.

Felt a little stiff this morning and yoga was a bit slow, but I think that it was the others there that I could feel. I've thought a lot about which feelings are really mine, I sometimes feel low and heavy, but then I wonder if that's really me or if I've picked up someone else's feeling. I think I'm carrying a lot and pick up a lot from people around me.

We did another thing after breakfast, we were supposed to see our own greatness and let go of our walls and barriers, i.e. be ourselves and not care about the judgement of other people. Considering the group that's here, there is no judgement. What we did was that each of us, one by one, had to sing a song. I'm used to singing so I didn't mind, and it wasn't a big deal, but it was exciting to see the others and what they thought. My insight today is to truly be who I am, not be afraid of judgements, take up space. A simple thing I thought about was that I sometimes get nervous when I am about to speak. Or that I talk fast or slur. I do that because I don't want to take up too much space, what I say might not be interesting, etc. But what I should do is to be calmer when I speak, believe in what I say and that it is just as interesting as what the others are saying. By being more myself, I will attract positive things and my greatness becomes even greater. I can grow as a person and become more interesting in the eyes of others, and by being true to myself I will feel better. I will allow my feelings to bubble up because they are just feelings. I will also discern whether the feelings are mine or whether they come from someone else. Feelings are just energies waiting to be released.

I realize that things will be a little different at home and I think that C will like it. I think this will make us stronger again. And it feels easy ☺
Enough for now.

I often write in my diary entries about being who I am, and to me that means allowing my feelings and thoughts and not judging myself. It doesn't mean I was a completely different person before, but that I accept on a deeper level that my thoughts and ruminations are okay. It is a part of me to be thoughtful, it is a part of me to be sensitive, it is a part of me to be able to pick up on other people's moods.

I now return to how I feel about and experience various social contexts. What became clear to me is how differently I experience different social situations. The amount of input and the risk of overstimulation are different depending on the situation. If I am on stage with my saxophone or presenting something to an audience, I can control the situation, prepare what to say, have expectations about how things will turn out, and decide what to do before and after. I thereby create an opportunity for recovery depending on the situation. When I talk to someone one-on-one, it is easy to get a feel for the other person and the conversation flows freely. But in larger social contexts, there can be too much input. If I am with colleagues, friends, or acquaintances, it can be overwhelming with everybody talking, and my own thoughts about what to say and what the others will think.

What does it mean to be brave enough? It is different for each of us. I have been brave enough to do many things, and some of them—like playing the saxophone on stage—are things that others would not dare to do. I have also *not* been brave enough to do a lot, including things that other people find not at all daunting. When I face new things that I haven't tried before, I become stressed and tense up. I guess this happens to a lot of people, but the risk is greater for highly sensitive persons because there is so much new information that has to be processed. Not just the thing in itself and how to do it, but thoughts about how others will react if you fail or succeed, what others expect, and so on. It has happened that I have avoided things because of this, or that I have become blocked in certain situations. I flee or focus on what I am good at instead of trying the new things that I am afraid of.

When it comes to men, this also has to do with norms about courage and not being a "coward." These norms can be stressful and make the situation worse. In my experience, there is an idea that "real" men are supposed to be good at practical things, and they should be bold and just go headlong into new situations. This has caused me to feel "wrong" in certain contexts, I have judged myself extra hard and avoided situations. Having the courage to do the things that I have done has probably been viewed as unmanly. My guess is that I am not the only man with these feelings.

For example, I never learned artistic gymnastics, which is a part of PE in Swedish schools. Don't ask me how, but I managed to get away with not doing it. I thought it was terrifying and I didn't even want to try. It also seemed as if everyone else already knew how to do it, and since I didn't, I was afraid to try. However, I suspect that many readers might have some degree of aversion towards gymnastics, so I will let another example show just how blocked a highly sensitive person can become when faced with a new and unfamiliar thing.

One time, I was with C and some friends on a sailboat out at sea. I had to go to the bathroom. When the skipper (my friend) explained how the toilet worked, I became stressed as there were so many things to do right; "First press here then press there, do this, do *not* do that." I got completely blocked. How was I supposed to understand all that, and what would happen if I did it wrong? So, I just noped out and thought, "I'm not going to the bathroom, I'll wait till we come ashore." It may seem like a ridiculous thing, but it illustrates what happens when you get overstimulated. It is a new situation and it feels like there is an almost infinite number of possibilities. There is too much information and you feel anxiety about doing it wrong. I can promise you that highly sensitive readers will understand.

Of course, I eventually worked out the toilet (after a little trouble) and I now use this experience to help me in similar situations. Whenever someone explains something new to me and I get stressed, I think, "Going to the bathroom on a boat" and that makes me aware of my reaction and my feelings, allowing me to calm down and solve the situation without acting out from fear or stress.

Day 3 Österlen, Saturday, August 27, 2016

Yesterday evening we had a meditation session where we slowly went through the whole body to find different emotions so that we could move on. One thing was to find the most painful emotion and get past that. What was the most painful thing that could happen? I couldn't think of anything and didn't find anything that powerful—but I felt a pressure over my chest.

This morning when I woke up the feeling of pressure over my chest remained. I woke around 4 am and my head was full of thoughts, but then I decided to continue the meditation to try and see what lay beneath. I felt that I'm afraid that it will hurt, so I shut down. That way, there's no pain because I've shut it off… and then the blockage came loose, and I let out the energy and cried. There is still something left though, and I feel like I need to really let go and have a good cry. When I was in bed, I held back so as to not wake my roommate.

We'll see what happens today, but it's good to let go a little bit. I realize that I've kept my sensitivity switched off for a long time. Now it's time to tear down the wall for real! It's almost time for a hike, we're all going on a trip, so I have to quit writing.

I remember that feeling very well, the thoughts about what would be the worst that could happen. That guided meditation stirred up a lot of emotions among the rest of the group. But I didn't get at those deep feelings at the time. The realization when I continued my meditation the next morning was incredibly strong: that it is the feeling of getting hurt that I am afraid of, the pain itself. I have been afraid to get close to people and then be let down and emotionally hurt. I have been afraid of getting hit and physically hurt. I was afraid to speak my mind, because I risked getting hurtful words back. The fear of pain had been so big and overwhelming, and I hadn't learned to feel and understand that the pain passes. Realizing that it is only a feeling and that it will pass was extremely liberating.

The research on HSP lets us understand that highly sensitive persons quickly learn to avoid pain and potentially hurtful situations. We learn what to do to make it right and then stick to that. We pick up on different situations and handle them so that we won't get hurt. During our childhood, we learn what kind of behavior works and then we shut off various feelings. The research also lets us know that sensitive boys put on a kind of armor during their childhood. I know that when I grew up, boys were supposed to "suck it up," be tough and don't be anxious about trying new things. I was anxious, thoughtful, afraid that things might hurt or that someone would laugh at me if I did it wrong. Hurtful words and not fitting in were very painful things for me. In hindsight, I see that I simply shut off certain feelings, and that I didn't learn to deal with or practice handling the bad things that might happen. How many of us have shut off our feelings?

I can remember many examples of this, and I think that many people can identify with them. I disliked physical violence, and I have never been in a fight because I was afraid that it would hurt, to get punched and experience the feeling of pain. So, I have avoided all such situations; I chose to walk away instead of standing up for myself. I have avoided tough discussions or arguments because there are so many hurtful words and accusations. I also remember being afraid of my brother; he acted out as a kid, had a short fuse and fought a lot. Now—with a little perspective—I know that my brother always meant well. He has told me that he got so mad at people who picked on those who were smaller that he stepped in and fought for them. As a kid, I didn't understand that, I just saw a brother who liked to fight. And I was afraid that it would hurt, so we never fought as kids—I was a true diplomat and made sure that there was never anything to fight about.

One of my biggest fears is close relationships. I have been incredibly afraid of getting close to possible girlfriends. Afraid of a "no" if I asked a girl out on a date, afraid to fall in love with a girl and then be rejected or dumped. I remember that my mother once talked to me about future girlfriends—I can't remember her exact words, but the gist of it was, "You've got to be lucky, Thomas, to find someone who can be with you, as complicated as you are." It was probably just something she let slip at one point when she thought I was being difficult, but it stuck with me. I told her about this not long ago, and she didn't even remember saying anything like that. That I took it so hard was probably because I already felt different.

When I was in middle school, I had a strong feeling that I wasn't the kind of person a girl would like to have as a boyfriend. I had many friends who were girls, I talked a lot with them and was—in that way— close to many girls. But I felt all the time that I was a friend, not a potential boyfriend, because I wasn't cool. I didn't do badass stuff, instead I was a softie. I recall one time when some girls in the ninth grade got the idea to set me up with another girl who was probably in the same situation as I was, and how they laughed, and I quickly left. Many things affected me and made me afraid of showing interest in a girl. But the thing that

I was most afraid of—and this has stayed with me for a long time—was that when I met a girl and she got to know me she would see who I really was. And when she saw who I really was she wouldn't want to be with me, and then she would tell everyone else what a weirdo I was. And then I would lose all my friends. Thus, I was somewhat ambivalent: while I easily talked with girls and had many friends who were girls, I was very afraid of getting together with any one of them.

This has had a very restricting effect on my life, and I haven't admitted it to myself until perhaps now, with the perspective I now have. Or perhaps it has been a gradual process. I can see now that from high school until I was in my thirties, I had my guard up, not letting myself get too close to people I met or became involved with. I realize that, whenever I was on a date or seeing someone, I chose to end it early on because it didn't "feel" right—but it was really all about me being too afraid to take the next step.

During my university studies in Linköping, seeing a whole lot of people came naturally, both at the university and in bars around town. I somehow knew that there was always a chance to talk again with the people I met on nights out. It was simpler somehow and I had a few shorter relationships, but I was never brave enough to get emotionally involved—instead, I backed off before I could be rejected. When I moved to Gothenburg at the age of 26, I had developed a self-destructive behavior. I hadn't had many girlfriends, and it became even harder to meet girls. I judged myself for not being more experienced: "What if I meet a girl now and she finds out that I haven't been with anyone for a long time, what will happen then?" I put expectations on myself, thought that I should know more, and it became a vicious circle. During this time, I partied a lot, especially on weekends. I made contact with girls and talked a lot, got their numbers, but then I couldn't work up the courage to call them. And so, I ended up in a weird situation: I wanted to meet someone, went to bars and tried online dating, but at the same time I didn't dare meet someone for real and open up to them. I was incredibly afraid of being judged or laughed at. But I didn't admit it to myself at the time; I kept telling myself that I hadn't met the right girl or that it didn't feel "right" being with the person I was currently seeing.

My friends moved in with their partners, there were weddings and couples' dinners, and I always felt like the only single. Then, when I was 29 years old, I met a girl and we were a couple for two years. It felt very good being in a relationship. And it was almost more important to be in a relationship than for the relationship to be one hundred per cent good. I knew in my heart that we wouldn't last, and we didn't move in together. But I also felt that this girl was in the same place as I was: we needed each other for the time being and we helped each other in many ways. But you could say that social expectations made me want to be in a relationship rather than break up and be single, even if it wasn't meant to last.

When that relationship inevitably ended, a lot happened inside of me. That is when I started to understand more and more about feelings. I began to follow my feelings more often, gained many new insights, and increased my self-awareness through various leadership courses. I also started going out with C at this point, at 32 years of age. We were on the same level, the same course in life, we were very allowing and under-standing of one another. We were friends before we got together and had talked a lot, and I had told her of my innermost fears. So, when we became a couple she provided a safe environment in which I was allowed to be insecure, and where I could talk about my thoughts and questions. It was very important for me then to be allowed to be that person, and it helped me grow immensely. We moved in together and for the first time, at the age of 33, I lived together with a woman. We got married a couple of years later. Sharing a home meant a new kind of challenge with being in a close relationship, and the next step in having the courage to talk about things.

The consequence of not allowing oneself—not daring—to feel is also interesting. If we don't dare to feel or to face the risk of being hurt, we miss out on so much. We miss out on close relationships because we don't dare go all-in and risk being hurt. We miss out on standing up for ourselves if we avoid all confrontations. By practicing and learning to understand how to handle emotions and how to let the pain pass through us, we can live more. We dare more and I believe that we can get more out of life that way.

Day 4 Österlen, Sunday, August 28, 2016

I'm sitting on the bench again, the last morning here this time around. Everything feels very good today, there's no right or wrong in my head and I laugh inside at how easy it can be sometimes. My thoughts about what I should do, they don't matter ☺ Go for the simple things. Listen to my awareness. Let the feelings come, they are just energies, I let them go and allow them to be. I let go of my wall and let others take my energy; I can just replenish it. There's no need to get tense. When I woke up, I went over a bunch of scenarios in my head: my job, being at home with my family, being with my parents—and it feels so good because it will all turn out well. I love it and it feels so liberating to just be and not worry about everything all the time and be so hard on myself.

After I wrote in my diary yesterday, I met Zara, one of the participants, who sat on this very bench. We started talking and it came loose, and I cried even more. We talked about pain and how it hurts so much. She talked first and I could identify with what she said, and it's so liberating and good to have someone else with the same thoughts, someone who understands me. Later, during the hike, another thing hit me: I felt limited by always adapting and I was both sad and angry. I was on my knees crying, beating my hands against the ground. I allowed my feelings to the fullest. It was hard right then—or maybe not—but it felt so good, and that pressure over my chest disappeared. And then I felt so good that I ran to catch up with the others, and I did whatever I felt like on that walk; I ran, walked, rested, and climbed trees. Climbing trees was a symbolic thing, because I remember not climbing trees when I was a kid since I was too afraid—but that was not my own feeling, that was my mother being afraid of me getting hurt.

Then we were supposed to throw five stones that we had carried with us, throw them off a cliff. The stones symbolized fears. This was also very emotional. I threw away the fear of being me, the fear of not being good enough, the fear of standing out and others thinking that I am weird, and two more that I can't remember. It was so good and liberating! When we moved on, I climbed trees and gave up a whoop of pure joy which inspired others to scream at the top of their lungs. That was a small signal to me to take the first step because others would want to follow. Then we all went for a swim in the sea and then back to breakfast.

I was a bit dizzy in the afternoon, felt that it had been a powerful discharge, but things are beginning to calm down now. I feel a profound serenity, I am happier and full of energy. Now it's time to gather with the group and I just heard thunder in the distance; apparently, it's going to rain today.

That feeling when I was on my knees beating the ground is one of the most powerful I have ever experienced. Early on during the hike I felt something stirring inside of me; very powerful feelings that needed to be let out. It was as if the experiences of these last few days—the opening of thoughts and feelings, allowing myself to feel the pain, that which I was most afraid of—all of it had to come out. So, there I was, on my knees and releasing my feelings, and it was an incredibly strong experience. It was also very good that our teacher was close by, because I really abandoned control and let everything out. It was actually like my whole life passed before my eyes when I fell to my knees, and it affects me even now as I am writing this. I felt a sadness—grief, even—over all the things I have missed out on because I have been too afraid and too limited: friends, new experiences, love. I have backed away in life so as to not stand out and I haven't received the joy that was there for me. I also felt anger for having done this to myself, and I asked myself why I hadn't realized this until now, why I have shackled myself. When the sadness and anger had been allowed to pass, there was calm, peace, and relief. I forgave myself; I now knew why I acted like I did and that would no longer stop me from living my life. The shackles had been broken.

The feeling afterwards was completely liberating. First of all, it had been very hard to let the feeling pass; I had never in my life experienced losing control and letting it just happen in that way. That I now had the insight that feelings are energies, that they disappear, that they only need to pass through my body, allowed me to fully experience the feeling. Afterwards the relief, freedom, and insight of what I had done were beyond compare. It might seem like a simple thing to run off to climb a tree, but for me in that moment it meant an incredible sense of freedom. My whole life I had chosen to limit myself, not letting myself be me, just so that I wouldn't stand out. To now experience that I could be myself all the way, that goes beyond words, it was an absolutely fantastic feeling.

The next challenge was throwing away the stones that symbolized fears, especially the one that symbolized the fear of standing out and others thinking I was weird. I held onto that stone for what felt like many, many minutes. It was hard just wording it, with the whole group behind me listening. It was a group I trusted but I was still anxious; what do they think of me now, what will they think if I say this or that. It was rooted so deeply, the fear of standing out. Giving the words shape and speaking them aloud was very hard. I cried. I fell to my knees and kept crying. I stood up and eventually that stone disappeared over the cliff edge—and so much inside of me shook loose. I couldn't believe I had been so afraid of standing out and being left out; it had followed me for so long. Laying myself bare and communicating my innermost fears to other people was incredibly hard but also amazingly liberating.

Letting go of things is also a gradual process. I was at a yoga retreat two years prior to this one and was in a similar situation then. But back then I didn't have the courage to be so honest with myself when I stood there with the stones in my hand. At that time, I wrote this in my diary: *Yesterday we went on a wonderful hike and we brought five stones that we were supposed to throw out into the sea. The stones symbolized things we needed to let go of. I had written a few things down but when I was about to throw the stones, I got stressed about what to say but I threw them anyway. I was nervous about making a mistake and that the others would think I did something wrong.* Back then, I was not ready to lay myself bare and admit what it was I really wanted to let go of. These things were deeply rooted, and it was a long process, but now they finally came loose for real. Gaining insights and working on personal development is a process; you realize and learn more about yourself gradually. It is like peeling an onion, layer by layer. When you think that, "Now I'm done," then the next challenge comes. I have been interested in personal development for ten years and I am still developing. It is all about being kind to yourself throughout the entire process, take the steps that you are ready to take and look under the stones that you can lift at that moment. I often think that we face the challenges that we are ready to face right now. I wasn't ready to throw that stone before because I was peeling other layers at the time—but this time I was ready.

The feeling that hit me as I beat my hands against the ground was so incredibly powerful, and I hadn't dared to share that experience with others before. Letting go, not being able to control it, not knowing what would happen. I later watched a documentary called *The Work*, a film about men in prison and free men going to joint therapy sessions. It is a very powerful film in which men share their feelings and fears. You can see how they gradually let go of years and years of dammed-up feelings. I especially remember a man who wanted to be able to weep for his dead sister. But he didn't know how to cry, he had never allowed himself to do it before. He was afraid of what would happen if he let go of his strict control. Whenever a powerful emotion like that had hit him before, he had assaulted someone. Now the group and the therapist helped him to let go of these powerful feelings that he had kept inside. It is a very strong scene when these feelings are allowed to surface; he screams and hardly knows what to do with himself. But he lets it all out and afterwards he is very happy and at peace. You can see on his expression just how relieved he is. Several others then experience similar processes. There is so much that has been kept in for so long. The question is how these men would have felt if they had learned to understand and manage their emotions earlier in life—and how that would have affected others around them.

It is somehow fascinating that so many of us will not allow ourselves to feel. We don't learn emotional management—or maybe we live life at such a fast pace today that we don't have time to feel. Regardless of why, we seem to think that it is wrong to feel, and we limit ourselves from living life to the fullest as emotional and sensitive human beings. I want to challenge you, the reader, to think about how you manage your emotions. How do you express feelings? Do you dare to feel? How do you learn how to manage and understand your emotions and feelings in a better way? Do you run away, or do you embrace the opportunities that come in your way? Are you being honest with yourself? Can you forgive yourself? And remember, your feelings don't have anything to do with any other person—they are your own feelings that you need to learn how to manage.

Monday, August 29, 2016

Back in Gothenburg, chilling on the couch. Julie (the dog) is sleeping next to me, I've got apples in the oven for apple sauce and C just got home from the gym.

It's been a very good day, I feel that I've had the tranquility I need, and I started the day with a little yoga. My wall has been down today and I breathe deep down in my stomach. It's been up and down but I've exercised and focused on my relaxation, and it's worked out well in meetings with colleagues and clients.

Talked to C this morning and told her what had happened, and it felt good, like she understood what I've been through. How does it get any better than this? ☺

Tuesday, December 6, 2016

It's been a couple of months since last I wrote. Things have been up and down, but mostly up. We went to the Canary Islands with the kids, and my mom and her husband Jan was there too. It was a great week in late October, but it was a drag to return home to the cold. But it felt as though my insights from the retreat in August have stuck, guess it's the kind of thing that sticks for life ☺ I have discussed a lot of good things since then, both at home and at work. I believe more in my own feelings, even if I—as I said—take it step by step. For example, I had a meeting yesterday with my boss and his boss, I brought up important matters but I sometimes still get blocked and things don't sink in until later when I get home. The good thing is that I learn about myself all the time. And the feeling of taking it step by step, expressing myself, believing in my feeling, it gradually increases my sense of security and my confidence. It's hard to describe in words, but for example, I had a tough week last week, four client meetings, almost one per day, I was incredibly focused and stable but felt that it was a lot. Then, on Friday afternoon, I was so pleased with myself and got such a great, calm feeling that it's hard to describe. It has a lot to do with my expressing my feelings and my beliefs, there is a certain stress and insecurity, but the more it works, the better it feels. I feel calmer both in speech and body language.

Met my former boss from Volvo Penta last week. She got me to realize what a journey I've made over the last year. From feeling so bad to exercising more, changing my diet, and working mentally with different methods to feel better. She said that I should really be proud that I've made this journey, and I was so glad to hear it. And it's good to reflect upon all that has happened.

It felt great to become stronger and stronger as the autumn went by. I took my new insights to heart and incorporated them in my everyday life. Naturally, things were a little up and down because I was changing my habits, but I let it take time, step by step. A major difference from before was my new perspective on things I did. Before, I was more worried about making mistakes, doing the wrong thing, and I judged myself and worried about many things. Now, I began to take it easy; I was kind to myself and allowed things to take time to settle. I had the courage to challenge myself, I followed my feelings and tried things out. How do you deal with new habits and change? Do you judge yourself if it isn't perfect right away or if you stray from the path once or several times? How do you deal with people around you when a new side of you emerges? What would it be like if you treated yourself like your best friend when you are about to learn something new or change a habit? To me, it was a big difference to be kinder to myself in this process. It takes time for things to settle. It takes time to change your perspective, your habits, or the way other people view you.

I finished the year by attending a rhetoric course as a preparation for an in-service training that I was going to manage at the company I worked for. It was a very good end to the year, practicing talking, getting feedback, and discovering that by being personal, the message comes across in an entirely different way. Highly sensitive persons are often described as insecure in social situations like at coffee break or parties and other larger gatherings. It was really valuable to practice talking in social situations and getting feedback on vocal pitch and so on. The most important thing that I took with me was to be calm in social situations. I mustn't get stressed about what other people might think, what they will think about the things I say, my fear of screwing up, and so on. I just have to stay calm and think that when I talk, it is my time to express myself—and then I can be personal and share my ideas. And even if someone finds it uninteresting or wants to interrupt and take up space, I must make the most of my time just as others take their time to talk. By being confident and having a steady voice, my message will reach those who are interested.

It is also interesting to see other people take up space and talk. I realize that we can all be nervous about speaking, not only us highly sensitive persons. That is reassuring. I also believe that if we are aware and respectful of not taking up people's time unnecessarily, and if we think about whether what we say fits into the conversation, and if we think before we speak, then our words will be of more interest to others. At the same time, our ideas and opinions are worth just as much as anyone else's. Imagine that we could express our feelings and opinions more without being so worried about what other people will think and say!

My life at this point was not so different when it comes to the things I did; the big difference was in the way I looked at life and things that happened. As I began to better understand my emotional patterns, I could take more responsibility for my own emotions and I could manage my experiences in a new way. I understood that my emotional reactions in the present depended on so much more—my history, my inheritance, dammed-up emotions—and that allowed me to be freer, to see things in a new light. It was *I* who chose my perspective on life and it was *I* who chose how to deal with things that happened in my life. It was a fascinating change of perspective. How I felt really had nothing to do with anyone else.

CHAPTER 8

Three Major Life Changes

Thursday, January 5, 2017

New year and new possibilities ☺ *I'm on the couch with Julie, it's shortly after 9 pm, we're going for a walk in a little while. I have a few extra days off after Christmas, C is working and the kids are on their way from their dad.*

My dad and his partner have been here for a couple of days, me and Dad went out with Julie yesterday and in the evening we all went out for dinner. It's always a bit tricky when they're here, things get a little tense, we try to socialize but it's a bit stiff. C thinks it's tough and asked me what we get out of it. And that's a good question, I suppose. Feels like my dad doesn't want anything, just to please us, and it gets tough when it all falls on me. But now I've learnt how to deal with it better and not be offended. But I want things to be good. Dad is a smart guy, I'll have to talk to him about what he expects and how he thinks we can make things better.

Am I like my father? In what way? What can I learn from that? What can I do better in my communication style?

Guess it has a lot to do with being yourself, being open, having opinions, sharing stories. And it's simple: just do it. Be genuine, listen, talk, and believe in what you do. That is what 2017 will be for me: joy, being who I am, taking my own time, and focusing on creating something. Challenge and create dynamism. I've held back for too long, and I now need to be more of me. And it is my journey. 2016 has been a year of recovery. I focused on my health and exercise, lost 12 kg in six months and kept my weight stable.

I exercise more regularly now, at least three sessions a week plus running. I eat better, no added sugar in over a year and it feels natural now. More vegetarian, light lunches, etc. Have worked on the mental stuff in 2016, reduced and prioritized my workload in order to focus and be at peace in my job. I must continue to have faith in my style, since it's working—I've taken it easy in 2016 and I still surpass the company goals ☺

So many crazy (or sound) things I did last year, little things that were big for me. Working out of a café instead of my office, going to the gym at lunch, having more space in my calendar, and not squeezing in a lot because I'm "supposed" to help others or because I "should" do more.

I realized that I had broken a pattern. I used to escape my feelings but in this last year, I dealt with them instead. For example, I hadn't worked things out with my former employers because I didn't have the courage to talk about how I felt or what I thought. Instead, I found new jobs and left the companies with a feeling that I didn't fit in and that they were glad to get rid of me. Now, I had a completely different feeling. I was more open and shared what was on my mind, I didn't hold myself back thinking that I was wrong; I took time to be with my colleagues and to pause. It felt incredibly good to break the pattern and realize these things.

At the same time, it felt great at home to realize that I am okay the way I am, to have the courage to break the pattern of always wondering if I am good enough. It had bothered me for many, many years. It was a great insight which made me more secure in being me. I felt an inner strength and I had the tools to handle different situations. I managed my feelings and thoughts with awareness, and I used questions to discern what it was I needed for the moment. I paused and broke negative patterns or overstimulation. When my thoughts started spinning, I went for a walk or something. A good expression that I began to use was, "I'm so tired that I have to go for a walk."

Saturday, January 14, 2017

This has probably been one of the strangest weeks I've ever experienced. At New Year's, C and I had some deep and heavy talks about us. How should we go on, how are we, should we continue together... Last year was a bit boring and we didn't feel the same spark as we did before. Simply put, we talked about separating if we can't find that spark again. It's tough as hell, but we had a good talk about why we've drifted apart. I'm on my journey and I've been bad at expressing what it is that I want. Been there for C, and it's been bad when I've felt like she's not appreciating what I do—but she hasn't actually asked for my help... Then I've felt like she has been distant and putting all her energy into things outside of home. She has tried to wait for things to feel good and I've tried to do all sorts of things to make it better. But what we really need to work on is our connection and that we can talk about and share everything again.

But, as I said, good talks, and it was tough but it also felt like we solved something. The week and weekend after were good, I took everything we talked about to heart and I understand that I've been boring and lacking in energy. But then, this Monday in the car driving from work, I felt that I've had it. I really tried after New Year's, but C always came back to her doubts and that we lack the spark. And then I felt that I'd had enough, I don't have the energy and I don't want to try any longer, so we decided that we're getting a divorce.

This'll have to be a cliffhanger; I need to go into town...

It was tough to realize just how far we had drifted apart. At the same time, it was good to act according to my insights from the previous year, about talking and being more open with what I think and feel. Instead of talking about how I felt, I had done things that needed to be done around the house or for her. I thought I was being kind and caring because I did these things. We had extended the house in the fall, and in that project we fixed a whole lot and did things we had talked about for a long time. But what we really did was avoiding the things we needed to talk about.

I think it is quite common to act practical and energetic when there is something missing from a relationship—it is easier to be practical and do stuff than to face the difficult feeling. It is often about fear, I think; you are afraid that the relationship will end, that you are not good enough, that things will be worse than they are right now. If you act on that fear it is often through flight/avoiding the problem, or by being aggressive/practical and energetic. But what if you could act differently and pause to consciously scrutinize the feeling? Then you could think that something is behind that uncomfortable feeling and that you have to face it, accept it, in order to move past it. To "hide" behind practical things just means you push the problem ahead of you. The feeling still remains, doesn't it?

To me, it was very clear—and painful—to realize how I had been avoiding talking about things. Instead, I "fixed" things, did tons of extra stuff to make our everyday lives easier, and I realized that I expected to be recognized for all the things I did and to get feedback or something in return. But if I do something for someone else, it is a gift, and when I give something to someone, I do it without expecting something in return—otherwise, it isn't a gift. But if I do something for someone else expecting to get something in return, it is going to be weird because they didn't ask for it. In almost the same way, it will be a weird situation if I say yes to doing something without speaking up if I actually don't want to do it. Then it will seem strange if I complain or expect something in return from the other person—I mean, I have said yes already. But if I am clear with how I feel and say something like, "I don't feel like doing that, can't we divide the work somehow?" then I am more honest, and we can agree on how to do it. It also becomes clear what it is I want, and I let the other person know that it can be hard for me. Before, I thought I was being difficult if I said no. That is often the case for us highly sensitive persons. We don't want to cause trouble or be difficult, we see what needs to be done and think that it deserves recognition when it gets done. But the other person might not even have known it needed doing. How then is it going to be recognized? It can be a good thing to think about what you do in your everyday life that you expect the other person to see. What kind of things do we give as a gift, all the while expecting something in return? What lies there, unspoken because we expect the other person to read our minds?

Sunday, January 15, 2017

Continuation to the cliffhanger... wow, what a week it's been... On Monday we decided to get a divorce and that was it. There was chaos afterwards; imagine being in the car on your way home and deciding that... And then the kids were at home so we couldn't continue the conversation. When I took the dog for a walk, it all broke loose, but it was good to be able to cry unhindered. I have become good at letting it out so that it doesn't get pent up inside. Anyway, I went home, slept poorly and woke up at 3 am. At 5 am, I got up and went out for an 8-kilometer run; I needed to get out and I cried at the end as I was getting close to home.

Then I had an early meeting, a breakfast meeting at 7.30. Had another meeting until 9–9.30, but then I just had to get out. My whole body screamed for solitude. I went for a walk down toward the opera house; luckily, I wore my winter coat with the big hood so no one could see the tears I released. Then I just walked and let all the feelings out; it was normal crying at first but then my whole body shook and my arms were tingling and it felt like there were little balls at the tips of my fingers. Scary, and it didn't stop but I focused on my breathing, thought that maybe I should call for an ambulance if I were having a panic attack or something, but then I thought again on focusing on my breathing and eventually it stopped. Afterwards I talked to Emil and that was a very good talk. I gained a little perspective and got to put things into words. I then felt like I need to take it slower and let everything settle down. I got to share Emil's perspective and he's a bit like C—just going straight forward—while his partner is more of the person who fixes stuff quietly. He told me about how he has perceived his partner and I could identify with that. After that I went and had lunch with my brother and we also talked a lot. I have to think about what it is that I want, where I will be in five years' time.

It felt better in the afternoon and at night I told C that I think we should give it more time. I don't want to throw away what we have too quickly, want to give it another chance and try to find the way back to what we've had. Especially considering the good talks we've had lately, and that we've understood what went wrong. So, it ended well anyway, and C agreed. Tuesday night was a bit calmer, but I still couldn't sleep well. The following days passed in a kind of quiet haze, I felt a bit numb but still happy and optimistic in a way. But then, on Friday afternoon, I got low again, called my mother and told her about the situation, got to release some feelings again, went for a walk. It was good to talk to Mom and get her input. She understood my perspective about me doing so much at home. It felt a little better afterwards, but I was rather exhausted from the emotional turmoil this week. But that night there was a party and dinner with the company. Not the best situation perhaps, but in some odd way I found some kind of tranquility inside. I felt that I talked more calmly, from a place deeper down in my stomach. I made more eye contact, dared more and felt more stable. I realize that that feeling was there earlier this week too. It's strange how I, in the middle of this emotional turmoil, found that tranquil place within. So, the dinner was good and I had fun with my colleagues. I took a walk home; we were at Nya Varvet so it was only a 30 min. walk. It was good to stretch my legs, and I got to release some more tears and feelings.

Saturday was quite calm, I was still in that tranquil place and felt like I could have more fun with the boys, just be myself again. On Saturday night we had a gig with the band, and we kicked ass. We had lots of fun and the people who danced enjoyed themselves. It was probably one of the gigs that I've enjoyed the most. When I had the lead melody or a solo, I went all-in. I felt great and had a lot of fun, focused on pitch and melody and it sounded great ☺

I'll go to bed soon but to sum up Sunday, it sank in that I've really started to be myself again. What happens now is that the heaviest part of

I had a feeling that I had lost myself and become boring. I had lost the fun in me and in my relationship. Many people can probably identify with this after a longer time with a lot to do. One example is the years with small children when things have to be done and there never seems to be enough time. Or is there time? It doesn't really matter if there is time or not, you have to talk about how you feel. I know people who have spoken clearly about it, "We're now in the years when we have small children, we're a team and we know it's going to be tough." They try to find little opportunities to just be together. They have found their way to talk about being there for each other. Other people I know have reduced their working hours to get the time they need. For example, both parents work 90 %, which means that one day each week, one of them is home with the children taking care of everyday things. However, it is not only during the years with small children that time can seem to disappear. It can be when you first move in together, or later in a relationship. You think, "This is how it should be; this is what my partner expects of me." At least, that is how it was when I grew up, the parental roles were clearly defined. And so, you adapt.

For me—and I guess for a lot of people—a lot of things had built up over many years. I was like a pressure cooker and little things annoyed me. And I didn't have the same energy to do things as I did before. I think many people can identify with this too. You act in a certain way when you don't recognize yourself. You get angry about small things, and things you used to do effortlessly are now difficult. Doing the dishes can seem like an insurmountable obstacle. How does this happen? By keeping many small things pent up inside, a lot of feelings are built up. It seems as if we sometimes think we are machines, and that we just have to perform tasks. But we are human beings with feelings and thoughts—and there has to be room for that too.

I can now see that my relationship with C had come to a halt, it had grown cold and I realized how it had gradually come to this. How I played a part in losing the spark between us. I thought that I shouldn't be difficult and bring up the little things that were on my mind. I didn't have the courage to talk about how I felt because I was afraid that it might cause a breakup or that it would arouse doubts or insecurity in C. But by holding myself back, I became an empty shell who just performed tasks. I didn't know who I was, how the emotional Thomas thought and lived. I was being practical, nothing more. At the same time, I stopped doing things that I needed to feel well, such as exercising and creating me-time. I felt that the relationship wasn't good enough and I tried to do more, but instead I almost smothered it by being there too much and trying to please her all the time. Obviously, I don't know exactly what the difference would have been if I had been more open and better understood what I needed, but at least I wouldn't have lost myself. If I had expressed what I needed and how I felt, then we could have talked about it. We would have been able to increase the understanding for each other and also the understanding of how we develop and think. It is my belief that a relationship becomes more alive when we are there for real and have the courage to be who we are. And by being that, we attract those who like us for who we are. Naturally, we are all different and have different needs, but to play a role in order to fit in doesn't work for anyone in the long run. It is unkind, both to others and to yourself.

If you do what I did and not bring up bad things in a relationship or at work, the conflict remains unresolved. I didn't express my feelings or opinions, didn't want to enter into the conflict. The result was that I suffered from burnout and that my relationship bore the brunt because I didn't have the courage to talk about my feelings. So, if we can defuse the conflict, have the courage to listen to our own voice, talk about things more easily, try to talk about the difficult stuff, then we can also feel better in the long run—both individually and in our relationships with other people. It is not about putting blame on others, but about bringing up and talking about the things as they are. "Now, the thing is…"; "Here's how I feel…"; "How would you like things to be in our relationship?"; "I need this to feel well, how would that work?" And so on. And imagine if it was completely okay to say, "I need to be alone for a while; it's got nothing to do with you, I just need a moment to collect my thoughts." How can you bring more of that kind of openness into your relationships?

Tuesday, January 24, 2017

C and I talked a bit tonight about how we feel, and I think it's better, but C still isn't feeling it. I get a little tired, and each time I hear it, it feels like I shut off a little bit more. So, I went to rehearse and talked with some of the guys in the band. Realized that perhaps I get too rational and shut off my emotions. Maybe I protect myself by not feeling all of it, but it might be limiting instead. So, from now on I'll feel all of it, dare to be the one who shows emotions and dare to become even more sad. Of course, I can't influence the way C feels, but I can influence myself. It can be that I don't feel, and it's probably true, I too am a little strained. It's something that's developed over time and it's not resolved in an instant. Guess I should always follow my feelings.

What you resist, persists. Wonder if C is resisting something that is now stuck? We'll have a chance to talk and feel more this weekend when we don't have the kids.

I now realized that I would regret it if I didn't allow myself to feel everything. Even if I should become sad or get hurt, or it should become painful, I would regret it if I didn't take the chance. By having the courage to feel, I knew that I was trying and that I would not later regret holding back. Because if I held back and we separated because of it, I would regret it.

How much we can miss out on if we are afraid to show what we feel! I guess many people can look back on similar situations, such as, "Why didn't I have the courage to ask that girl or guy out to coffee or a date?"— to not have the courage to take the first step towards something that seemed daunting at the time but now, with perspective, was a small thing. For me, there is especially one thing that reminds me to have the courage to take a chance. When I studied at the university, there was a girl there—we can call her Emelie. In my mind, Emelie was the sweetest, most beautiful and lovely creature in the world. I got to know her a little; we talked sometimes, ended up next to each other on the occasional lunch. There was tension there, but I never had the courage to ask her out. For two whole years she was right there, and I didn't take the chance. Now that I look back on it, I ask myself why I made such a big deal of it. What was I so afraid of? The worst thing that could have happened was that I got a "no" and then I would have known. I use this episode as an example when I need to summon up the courage to do something. For with several years' worth of perspective, this was a pretty small matter. It is somewhat similar with C; I wanted to have the courage to feel and give it everything right then. I didn't want to look back in a few years and regret my actions—or rather, inactions. What kind of examples do you have that can help you find courage today?

Sunday, January 29, 2017

We have decided, we're getting a divorce. It's tough but still okay. We talked this morning and C said something like, "We might as well separate now." She said that she doesn't feel anything anymore, I've wanted to try and get back to that spark, but now it's time… So sad this morning, but we went out for coffee before lunch, took Julie out for a walk, then I was sad and low again in the afternoon. Then we went to yoga class together at half past four. Very good yoga session and time for reflection. Very much up and down, but now we have decided, and it feels pretty good somehow. It's going to be tough to break it to the boys. Feels okay but right now I'm just empty and can't write anymore. Over & out.

I had seen a therapist in January. It was very good to talk, and she provided me with different perspectives and ideas. She listened when I talked about what had happened and about the insights I had gained the year

moment. And so, I have a hard time deciding right away when I get the invitation, because I feel that I must stand by my decision if I make one. I believe that this is an important aspect to know about, especially for those who are not highly sensitive persons but have friends or relatives who are (which most people probably have).

Thursday, March 9, 2017

Early morning, it's 6:15 am and it will be time to get up soon. I moved last weekend, it was very intense with all that needed doing, cleaning, throwing things away, renting a car, getting a storage unit, etc. On the moving day we went on from 10 to 3, getting everything here, going to the recycling site to get rid of some things, and then going to the storage unit I have rented. Completely exhausted after that and on Sunday I was a wet rag. Felt very empty, both from the exhaustion leaving my body and from the realization that I had actually moved... Have gotten hold of a beautiful apartment, perfect location, but everything is just so weird. C and I haven't spoken since Saturday. The moving day was okay, and it was a beautiful hug before I left on Saturday.

It feels so strange, I'm thinking that I should call but also that I don't want to. She has been clear about not wanting anymore, she's not willing to try. If we were to meet today, we wouldn't become a couple because we're too different. I sap her energy because I don't follow her ideas immediately and want what she wants, and still I think, "Shouldn't she be able to move past that?" Feels like she's built up an image to strengthen her decision, because I listen to her feedback, but a major part in it all is the fact that we've had a tough time together and I haven't been well... But what do I want? Do I want us to get back together? Did I like it? Right now, I don't know, it's just empty and hard. Got to continue to take it day by day and go for whatever feels good at present.

Yes, we'll see what happens. We'll see each other this weekend when I'm taking J to the bandy game and meeting the guys. It's good to have some plans anyway, and also that there's room for relaxation and reflection...

I chose a sublease for the time being. I actually got the tip at the bank when I was applying for a loan commitment. The bank woman had also separated recently and told me to not make too many decisions at once, that I should find some space and settle for a temporary living arrangement. After the bank meeting, I checked online for apartments and applied for a couple. Later that week, a woman called me regarding a sublet in Eriksberg, a district in west Gothenburg. After we had talked a little, she asked me where I lived because she recognized my voice. It turned out she owned the hair salon in my neighborhood and had cut my hair a couple of times. What a great coincidence! I went to see the apartment and it was nice, furnished, close to the water and with a patio. Just what I wanted, open, calm, and airy. It felt really good, we agreed, and I got to rent it for the time being. I could move in after only 2–3 weeks. It felt great to get away from all the difficult stuff and get the pause I needed.

It was obviously tough to move out, to go through all the stuff and decide what to keep. But it was still good to do it, rip off the band-aid, and then get to a place of my own. Yet it was incredibly hard to wake up alone on the first morning, in an empty apartment, no kids, no animals, no C by my side. Great emptiness, many thoughts, but also a sense of serenity. Changes are naturally tough, but I had to take it step by step and allow myself to be sad.

Tuesday, March 21, 2017

I'm low, sad, everything just feels empty. I'm alone in the apartment, boring day at work, did have a fun rehearsal with the band though, but just empty and sad…

Read a book this weekend about behavior and analysis of different personality types. It was clear what kind of behavior C has and what kind I have. And the sick thing is that I can understand C's behavior, and mine too. But her forwardness, and in my opinion aggressive behavior, is just her way of showing that she wants something. She wants things to happen and just goes for it, it's not that she means to cause hurt, she just wants it to happen. My behavior is the opposite and I grow quiet and angry without showing it. It's so easy to be wise in hindsight...

I want to talk to her, shake her, and make her understand. Thought about calling but talked to my friend Emil and realized that I should wait a bit, it's not the right time. Or is it? What is it that I hope will happen? That she changes her mind? That she says, "I'm sorry" and that we'll try again? Do I want to try again, or do I just want things to be like they used to? If I can't answer that, it's probably best to wait a while. I'll focus on what I need now. I realize that my work also steals energy, I'm just waiting for the right moment and then I will quit and start my own business. I really feel that it's time to cast off and try something new. It's going to be fun, although I don't know exactly what will happen, but that's the exciting part.

Time to sleep, feeling a bit better now ☺ Sleep well and a big hug to me!

I managed day by day even though it was tough. I allowed the difficult feelings to be felt because I knew that they would eventually pass. This was a phase I was going through and if I postponed it, it would only take me longer to get through it; it couldn't be avoided but had to be dealt with. In this new phase, I also chose to listen to my body in order to understand how best to deal with the difficult feelings. I chose to avoid alcohol, TV, and drowning myself in mindless input. This was in the spring, so I went for a lot of walks (often both mornings and evenings), went out into nature, took it easy, and wrote and reflected a lot. This worked for me, and it is important to find your own way to deal with grief, but remember to allow it and not avoid it, because you have to deal with it in your own way. To not deal with your emotions is like trying to escape your own shadow.

Some days when it had been extra heavy, the feeling came as I drew closer to the apartment. I felt heaviness and crying coming in my chest and throat. But now I knew my own body well enough to know that I had to vent my grief. As I stepped off the ferry or bus and began to get closer to home, the feeling grew stronger and stronger. I had to get inside and let the feeling play out. I unlocked the door and barely had time to take off my jacket before I started crying. It was such a relief to vent everything I had kept inside during the day. I sank back against the wall in my hallway and sat down on the floor. I gave way to everything that had to come out; I cried and cried, letting everything go. It passed after a while; I felt lighter and was able to stand up. It is a very difficult moment when you vent your grief, but it feels so good afterwards. I tried to find opportunities to cry because I knew I needed it. To me, crying is my body's way of venting emotions. At this time, I was teaching a class two mornings a week, and when I got to my car at lunch, I got that break. I did my job and taught the class, but in the car, it was time for me and the tears again.

Sunday, April 2, 2017

Started the day by going for a run, great to get out in the morning! It's now 10:30 and I'm having coffee at Da Matteo, great Sunday ☺ Party for J today who turns 11, big guy! The boys were here yesterday and we went hunting for Pokémon and had a fika[5] at my place.

But wow, what a week! Quit my job on Monday. Guess my boss wasn't completely taken by surprise, but he naturally said he was sad to see me go. Such a tension that was released, I was nervous when I spoke to my boss but afterwards it was like I was high. It went out to everybody at the company on Tuesday and many colleagues have been in touch to ask what I will do now and to express that they think it's sad that I'm leaving. I'm very happy and thankful that so many ask and are curious about what I will do.

---

5   In Swedish, a *fika* is a situation in which people get together, usually over a cup of coffee and a bun or piece of cake, to talk and socialize. As a verb, the word means 'to have a coffee', 'to hang out'. As a noun, it means both the getting together and the things you eat and drink—for example, if someone asks, "Should I bring fika?" it means, "Should I bring buns or cookies?" It is very common for coworkers in Sweden to have a fika together, and it has a more social function than a regular coffee break, as you often sit down to socialize instead of just exchanging a few words around the coffee machine.

Feels like a lot of people are impressed that I'm taking this step to try something new and start my own business—I guess many people dream of doing that. Feels absolutely right, I've been calm the rest of the week and I feel that this will work out fine. I do have a security in that I have a year's worth of salary in the bank. I also have an incredibly strong will to make this work and to make it fun, I will initiate meetings, follow my feelings, and do everything with great energy. A good feeling of gradually doing what I believe in. Not be stressed and thinking that everything has to be done quickly, but let things take time. One stress factor is gone, that I didn't have the energy to begin because it felt insurmountable. I'm calmer and more focused in everything I do now.

The separation and everything new, it's all beginning to settle. I'm not as sad anymore, I begin to look ahead but I'm still taking it day by day. Starting to see some more friends again, the ones I feel I can see now. That's what it's about now, being brave, making contact and believing in myself, and taking it easy. And another thing, having the courage to be open. I have been very open with how I feel and I've seen how much I gain from that. So, I'll continue to be open, talk about stuff that comes up, not think of what I "should" say or keep things to myself. Life is too short for that. Looked back a little at what I wrote about two weeks ago. It's incredible how things can change—now, I don't want to fix things with C. I want to look to the future, do what I want, be happy, follow my feelings and do a lot of fun stuff, grow as a person, challenge myself. Just think about everything I've shut off to please others and because I've felt like I'm not good enough and not loved. Now, I will deal with things and not be intimidated if they take time or feel difficult—if I don't start, I will never finish anything. I create my own future through my own actions!

That's all for now!

I was now very open with how I felt when my friends and colleagues asked me. By being this open and telling them how I truly felt, I got closer to them. If they expressed an interest and asked me questions, I would talk about the separation and my thoughts about everything that happened. I talked about how C and I drifted apart, about my image of how I—unfortunately—distanced myself, how we lost our spark and how we stopped talking like we used to. I noticed that people identified with what I said and they began to reflect on their own relationships and where they stood. I could tell from their behavior and thoughtfulness that they would bring this home to their respective relationships. They got a positive eye-opener. At the same time, they shared their own experiences and talked about similar situations that they had been through. I used to think that I was alone with my thoughts, but the more I shared with friends and colleagues, the more I realized that many of them felt the same, as they opened up. I appreciated the more relaxed mood and that we really talked about what mattered most in that moment. We got closer to each other, and for a brief moment we shared a beautiful understanding and concern for each other. I think the proverb "shared grief is half the sorrow" is something more people should take to heart. It is a kind of mutual trust that comes with letting yourself be vulnerable: two people who give each other space to talk and to listen. That space in which you are able to share your thoughts when things are tough is part of the essence of being vulnerable—and strong.

At this point, I also chose to take the leap and start my own business. I had thought a lot about this, whether it was too much change at once, but I felt that it was time. It was so good to finally take the step. I think that sometimes you can get stuck in a mindset that tells you that things should be difficult and that you are supposed to be sad and low. For me at this time, it was a kind of double deal: on the one hand, I allowed myself to be sad but on the other hand, I was having fun. I wanted to create things because it gave me energy; if I became passive and just brooded and felt low, then I got stuck in that mindset. By allowing myself to do both at this time, I allowed my grief to be processed while also fueling up with energy and being creative, and I moved forward and created new opportunities for myself.

with them and to go for walks with Julie. It felt a bit weird to be living in the house, it's emptier there now even if most things are the same. Then when I was about to leave, I got a bit emotional and sad, don't know what it was, perhaps it was the similarity with the last time I left, or maybe I was just sad to leave a second time. Don't know for sure, but when I got sad, Julie came to comfort me ☺ I think maybe it was because it was tough to go and leave the animals. But it's been a couple of weeks since I last was sad.

Otherwise, I'm still recovering and reading the book "Being You, Changing the World" by Dain Heer, which I picked up at the yoga retreat, and it's good to be reminded of things and thoughts.

A simple difference, perhaps even a small one, but I have become calmer when I speak, and better at looking people in the eye. Realize that I have been avoiding that, don't know for how long… But now, I feel a difference and look people calmly in the eye when they speak or when I talk about something, and it feels good. I feel right away that we connect better, and it gives me energy. Met an old trainer that held a sales course I took, and he talked much about eye contact—and now, considering the book I'm reading, it feels absolutely right.

A lot is based on being myself and being comfortable with it. Especially now with work, I feel calm, and the same goes for my upcoming trip. I'm going alone, both on the trip and in my business, and it feels like a lot of people wonder and say things like, "Wow, are you going by yourself?" and "You'll have a lot of work building your own business" and "Do you have any assignments now that you launch?" Sometimes it feels like I'm apologizing for not having jobs and assignments ready, but I await the autumn, and traveling by myself feels good. And then I realize that it's more about their worries than my own.

Thinking about one thing in the book I'm reading, to really do what feels good and not fulfil expectations about how I "should" act or feel. There is so much I have done to adapt. Now, it feels great and also challenging to let go of the control and just follow my feelings. I have many leads on assignments but nothing is set right now, sure it can be a little stressful, but at the same time I have planned for this and have enough money in the bank to go a full year without work. So, it's a bit crazy to be too worried, I've got food on the table and a roof over my head, even if I don't have any assignments. But, I mean, I will get assignments, I just don't know where yet ☺

Sunday, May 21, 2017

What a week!!! Friday was the last day at my old company, had a nice farewell fika, my boss gave a beautiful speech, and my colleagues had many nice things to say. The whole week was special, didn't have that much to do, most of my tasks had been handed over already, so I have been able to spend time with colleagues and fix other things.

I've also taken the boys to a concert, had a meeting with the housing co-operative where we did some fixing-up of the property, and then yesterday it was the Gothenburg Half Marathon and a post-run dinner at my place the same night. Yes, it's been a busy week… ☺ Feels great, even though I was feeling a bit under the weather prior to the half marathon. I think it was stress or something, had a little bit of a sore throat and felt a heaviness in my chest, but the race went well anyway, and I finished in 1 h 57 mins.

Today will be a quiet day for reflection and recovery. I'm also looking forward to next week with my trip to Rome on Tuesday night and I will stay till Sunday. It's also going to be great to get started with my new business, to build something, meet new people, and do what I believe in and feel passionate about, it's so exciting! ☺

What a year so far, and last year too with all the insights. I've been see-ing C a little lately and it's fun to get together. A little unsure of where we stand. I was there on Friday and the hugs when I came and went were a little warmer. It felt good and I start to think that perhaps there's something there, but I'll take it easy. I'm here if they need me, but I'm focusing on my own stuff. Taking every day as it comes, no stress about meeting someone new. I feel good and will have fun, and when it's time for something new, it'll come along.

better what I want. I want to travel, start my business, get going, have fun, and I can hang out with C, but we don't have to get back together. I want to meet new people, network, and experience new encounters.

It felt great that I could now bring up the things that were on my mind. Instead of thinking, making up stories, and guessing about what might happen, I asked. Before this, I used to go around and think a lot back and forth, even making up another reality. And I might even have become angry or disappointed about what she meant by that warm hug and then growing cold. Why did she do that? I would think like that and thus create drama that didn't actually exist. Imagine how much suffering and brooding we can avoid if we instead talk and ask questions. I used to be afraid of how the other person would react, maybe with anger, or make fun of me, or laugh it off, and so on. Now, I instead think that if I am open and honest, I will get my answer either verbally or between the lines. If they get angry or I notice that they can't deal with it, I know where they are coming from; their reaction is an answer in itself. And that they don't know how to deal with it, is their own challenge and not mine. It is not my problem; I am confident with being open and honest. By asking questions, you don't have to guess; you get answers, spoken or unspoken, and you can move on.

Thursday, June 15, 2017, continued

I'm psyched about going to Spain, leaving on Tuesday and it's going to be a seven-day hike on the El Camino. Thought about this a long time, that it would be fun, and now I'm doing it, booked a trip to Bilbao and have now purchased everything and planned my packing. It's going to be great to get away. Tried a hike yesterday, 11 km, and it felt great. But wow, my mind is racing; how should I plan the trip, optimize, what should I do when I get there, am I doing the right thing, should I do something differently. But then I feel that I just need to take it easy, the trip there doesn't have to be optimized, I don't need perfect housing, I won't miss out on things and have regrets. The important thing is that I go, try, and actually get away and learn, this is a first and a learning experience. So now I've booked flight, bus and taxi to Saint Jean Pied de Port. Once I get there, I'll find some place to stay the night and decide whether or not to walk on day one.

Otherwise there is a lot to do with getting the business started. But the most important thing is to keep calm, focus, and be myself. It feels great to really be able to focus on my own stuff and I feel that it's working out well, I'm having fun and getting close to people. Feels like it's a practice phase now, have different meetings, always remain calm, believe in myself, and become stronger. When I'm really there, it feels great, but then I get tired too, but I guess that's okay, it's always a bit uncomfortable before new things and habits settle. I'm on the right track anyway...

I had thought about going hiking in Spain for quite some time. When I was taking my usual walk one morning in May, I saw two people getting off the ferry. They both had big backpacks and when I got closer, I saw that the pilgrim scallop shell adorned their backpacks. The scallop shell is a symbol for the pilgrimage that all Camino hikers wear. I wanted to know more so I stopped and asked them if they were returning from Spain. And of course, they had just come home from a month of hiking along the El Camino. I told them I was thinking about going but hadn't decided yet. They spoke highly of the trail and the experience and told me to go. I took it as a sign and when I got home, I immediately booked a flight to Spain. Step one was to book the trip, everything else could be handled later. The main thing was that I went.

It was as if something was released when I booked the trip. Before I booked it, it was as if all those unsure things that I didn't know how they would play out kept me back. I envisioned tons of different scenarios. What will it be like to live in hostels? Will I be able to do all that hiking? What kind of things should I bring? Will I do it right? But that all went away when I booked the trip and thought that this is exactly the kind of thing I need to practice. Letting go of control and letting things take time, having the courage to try and see what it brings. The fact that I think so much and ponder all the options have kept me from doing things in the past. But with this hike, I would take it step by step. I would try it and see what it was like. I asked for help when I purchased all the things I would need; I guess I was in the store five or six times to buy more stuff.

In general, I think that new things have been stressful for me in the past, especially because of my need for control and knowing how things will play out. It is the same thing with new clients; I want to do so much, and I can see how I can help them. And that can be stressful. I have to let it take time instead, be calmer and more myself. I can't control everything that is going to happen, and it is difficult and stressful to try. What I can control is myself, and that means I can go along with and adapt to what is going on.

CHAPTER 9

New Life Perspectives—El Camino

Wednesday, June 21, 2017

I'm sitting in a courtyard outside the hostel in Roncesvalles. Had a long journey yesterday, left home at 4:30 am, the flight was at six, we made a stopover in Amsterdam and then landed in Bilbao at 11:20 am. Then I took a bus to Pamplona at 1 pm, and it was a two-hour ride. A taxi picked me up at 3 and I arrived in Saint Jean Pied de Port at 4:30 pm, so it was a long day. Had a great conversation with a Finnish guy on the bus, and I also talked a lot with the taxi driver. Once in SJPDP, I met a girl from Austria and we hiked to Huton, roughly 5 km and a 700 m altitude difference. It took around two hours and it was really hot. But still good to get there.

Today has been a great day, with an incredible view of the Pyrenees. Started at around 6:30 am to a beautiful red sunrise, seen sheep, horses, and cows, plus a lot of hikers of course. An okay day exertion-wise, arrived at 1 pm. Started out with a couple of other people, but then I walked alone for a while. I've talked with a lot of people. Sandra from the US during the hike, then an Australian at lunch, and then a group of people outside the hostel. A lot of fun even if I was a bit tired at lunch, probably didn't drink enough water. But a lot of fun conversation, and it was simply fun to talk. Felt great when I walked, such a sense of freedom, so happy that I did this, that I'm actually here, so proud of myself.

Thursday, June 22, 2017

Another great day, started at 6:15 am and arrived at 12:30 pm, a hot day again so I decided not to go on to the next village, so stayed in Zubiri. Today I've talked a lot with a guy from California, a philosophy student who has just graduated. We are very likeminded, although he is 24 years old, and I shared my own journey from insights to yoga retreats. We talked almost the entire day as we walked. It feels as if he is a highly sensitive person too and has similar thoughts and doubts. Feels as though he got a lot out of talking to me and I increasingly feel that this is right. He really appreciated our conversation and I'm very happy to be able to share, and it strengthens my resolve to be myself and share my experiences.

Did some yoga by the river after the hike, and it was great, but I still got emotional and cried a little. It was when I felt how happy I am to be on this journey. I like it so much, I'm talking to lots of people, everybody is open and sharing. At first, it felt a little unfamiliar to be talking like that, but now it's better and better. And I'm relaxed and trying to take it easy and do whatever I feel like, and that's very good.

How great is it that I'm actually here doing this! Feels so good! That's all for now!

It was a very liberating experience to go on this pilgrimage, and it was fun to meet new people again. One interesting aspect of being on a trip like this is that the people you meet don't have an image of you, no preconceived idea of who you are. You can test your ground and get a fresh start. It was especially interesting to talk to the guy from California. I could identify so deeply with his story, and my thoughts and feelings were the same when I was his age. It was almost as if I were talking to myself. I felt that I could contribute to his thoughts and ruminations. I also noticed that it was easier to talk when it was just the two of us, and no women were close by. He seemed to open up more then. He told me about how he felt that he was playing a role in his current relationship, how important it was for him to be in a relationship, and how happy he was that someone actually liked him. We talked more and he related memories from when he was growing up and how he felt that his parents really didn't want another child, but he was born anyway. In his experience, he wasn't really liked. His brother was the athlete, the successful guy who had all the girls. He didn't have the same interests, but still tried to live up to that role which he didn't fit into. I am grateful that he shared this with me. We also talked about how he wanted things in his current relationship, and how he would talk with his mother to get past the tense relationship he felt they had. It was emotional for him to share his story and he was very grateful for our conversation. At first, I felt a resistance from him about opening up but when I shared my story very openly, the mood lightened, and he began to talk more. For me, it was a great experience to be there for him, and it got me thinking, "Can my story contribute to other people's lives?"

On a journey like this, it is easy to see that the people you meet are very curious about who they meet. There is an openness and a genuine interest. Most of the people I met were on that journey for a reason, they had chosen to do the pilgrimage and they knew what it meant to hike. That was important, the fact that the people there wanted to open up and get as much out of the experience as possible. It is interesting that we need to go on a journey to be open towards people when we meet people every day. The biggest difference I noticed was the presence in those who had already been on the trail a while. You could see it in their eyes, they were relaxed, they lived in the present, and wished everybody well. Early on, when I talked to two French women who had that *presence*, I immediately felt that I wanted that too, it seemed so genuine.

Saturday, June 24, 2017

This morning we started at 5:30 am, I tagged along with a couple of others who wanted an early start. Good talks and when we reached the top of the hill with the pilgrim sculptures, I stopped a while by myself. There were feelings that I needed to vent. I sat down and meditated for a while, had that same sense of joy about being here. The woman I talked to on the way up was very positive and told me I brought a beautiful energy with me when I came to a group, and that made me very happy to hear, and it strengthens my resolve even more to continue to be who I am.

And it was a little odd on the summit when the tears came, that there wasn't really a feeling, it was just tears that needed out. I think it's because I'm happy, or rather, I know. I'm so glad that I'm doing this. Okay, continue later!

Saturday, June 24, 2017, continued

Arrived at the hostel around 2 pm, a different day from the rest. Strong emotions at the summit where I meditated, then I walked alone for the major part of today's leg. Didn't think much, just kept walking, and it felt good to walk alone. It was a bit odd that I didn't think of anything special, but that I just walked. Then when we arrived at the village, I had to just walk away and be by myself, and more was released, and I cried a bit more.

Then a quiet afternoon, we had dinner at the hostel and it was great. Good food and wonderful staff. I haven't rescheduled my flight home yet, but I think I will so I can walk five more days and get to Burgos. I don't think or feel anything special now, will just go to bed.

It was a very powerful moment when I was on the top of the hill by the statues symbolizing the pilgrimage. I had thought about walking the trail for so long, it had been a very intense spring, and I had been worried about the trip. I felt a very powerful sense of gratitude towards myself for finally doing this. The nice people I met, all the good chats, and nice words made it even more powerful. It was an intense experience followed by a great sense of relief.

Sunday, June 25, 2017

I'm in a church in Estella, taking a little time for reflection. Met a Dutch guy and we talked about presence and that you don't always need words to understand each other. He had an example from Tibet, where he had met a monk whom he couldn't talk to, but they met several times, and through glances and body language they could understand each other. I'm thinking that I often stress, I want to push forward and quickly add my opinion, idea, or story. I need to take it easier and just let it take time.

Monday, June 26, 2017

Yet another day, and I walked about 21 km today. The plan yesterday was that we would walk to a monastery, but we were misinformed and the monastery was not where we thought it would be. So, we arrived at another big hostel where we were going to stay. But I got a feeling that I didn't want to stay there, so I decided to walk on alone. Met an Irishman, Paul, and we walked together to the next village, five km away. We arrived in a lovely little village and found a hostel with just eight beds. It was very nice, vegetarian, and organic. Later, I found out from three American women who had checked in at the first hostel that they were not happy with it as it was big, next to a sports center, and noisy. At 6 pm, the three women decided to check out again and move on, and they ended up in the same place as Paul and me. So happy I followed my feeling and walked on.

It feels so good when I walk too, because I usually don't think of anything in particular, I just walk and don't think at all. And yet I cry a little now and then, things that are released somehow. It's like what an Italian lady who is on the hike said, "By walking, you melt the snow in your body"—i.e. by simply walking, things are released.

I have now rescheduled my flight and will leave a week later, so it's going to be a 13-day hike instead of a 7-day, feels great! So, I'll just continue and take it day by day.

It was as if Paul personified what I needed in terms of pausing and walking more calmly. During the spring, there was so much to do with the divorce, housing, and the new business. I felt stressed even when talking, and about all the things I wanted to do. Now, I ended up with Paul who was the slowest hiker of all. But despite walking the slowest, he didn't usually arrive that much later at the end of the day. If we did a leg of 20 km, it took Paul maybe 20 to 30 minutes longer to get there, and that isn't a big difference when you walk 5–6 hours a day. It gave me a perspective on pausing. I could enjoy nature more; I noticed more details and enjoyed the whole day more. It wasn't just a long haul to get to the next goal. I guess that has often been the case for me. I fight to reach the goal as soon as possible, to get done so I can relax, but I miss out on the experience on the way there. I think that many people can identify with this; we are supposed to do so much, and we run so fast that we don't enjoy life itself.

I met the Italian lady Bilo on the second day of the hike. She was a wonderful woman in her sixties with incredible energy, and her expression, "By walking, you melt the snow in your body," really hit me. When Bilo entered a room, it was illuminated by her joy and curiosity. She told me that she goes hiking one month each year. She has walked several different trails around Europe, along the coast of Portugal, in northern Spain, and one from England all the way down to Rome. She said that the break, the time for reflection, and the people that she met on these hikes meant a great deal to her. She walked alone and used the long vacation she had because she was a teacher; her husband stayed at home and her children were grown up and had moved out. The most important lesson I learned from her was that sometimes it is enough to just walk. Put on your shoes and go outside; by simply moving your body, you help yourself let the heavy stuff melt and drain off.

Tuesday, June 27, 2017

I'm now in Logroño, started at around 6:30 am and arrived at 12 pm. Walked with Paul from Ireland, so we took it easy and today we walked 20 km. Tomorrow it'll be a little longer, around 30 km. There are some longer stretches between villages/cities, so the length of the legs differ.

Yesterday evening, I practiced being myself at dinner and afterwards, it felt great and went well. I listened a lot and made good connections with several people in the group whom I felt were a bit noisy, but I kept to mine and it felt good.

Now we're going out for dinner, I'll be back!

That evening, I tried being calm with a bunch of Americans who had a lot of energy. I think it is easy (even for non-highly sensitive persons) to fall into other people's patterns, let their mood or noise level affect you—perhaps you have also noted that you may even change your own dialect to mimic a person you are talking to and whom you look up to. Or that you make jokes that you otherwise wouldn't because the group does it. I sometimes unconsciously adapt to other people's pace and jargon, and I can get exhausted afterwards because I have tried so hard to fit in. As I said, it is easy for this to happen, but I think it could be valuable to try and be aware of it and actively choose not to adapt—to follow your own way and see where it leads. That is what I did that evening with the Americans. It made me feel calmer and then we had a very interesting discussion. One of the guys began to talk about his time as a volunteer worker in Jamaica. I noticed that his friends hadn't heard all of it before, and I felt that my calm, my questions, and me being me allowed him to talk about it. I felt full of energy afterwards, and the experience strengthened my resolve to not play roles but be myself.

Wednesday, June 28, 2017

We're about to go out for dinner, and I'm waiting in reception. Another great day, started at 6 am from Logroño, had a coffee and then walked 13 km to the first stop where I had breakfast. It was a two-and-half-hour hike. Walked alone today, needed it, during the first leg some feelings about the separation bubbled up, about me not bringing up how I felt and the consequence of that. It was released and I cried a bit, good to vent it. At the first stop, I had coffee, juice, and a bocadillo, talked to a woman from England and a yoga woman from the US.

My thoughts today have been about continuing to relax; a conversation doesn't have to be perfect; if I say something, I don't always have to expect a certain reply. The same things come back, being myself, taking it easy, talking calmly, giving it time.

Then another thing, a little bit like yesterday—don't go into other people's energies, be aware of them but remain in my own sphere. At the end of the hike I felt a heaviness over my chest and in my throat. Didn't know what it was but then I realized it was a woman I had walked behind and passed a couple of times, an overweight woman who was having a tough time, and I picked up on her energy, realized that after a while and then it disappeared. It's interesting how I get a feel for such things so clearly.

Found a hostel and I realize how my values have changed, as it felt like a luxury to get a room with ONLY four beds… ☺ I usually want my own place, realize it's one thing I've become better at, living with other people, sleeping in a bunk bed, sharing bathroom, etc. It feels completely natural and simple now. To only have your backpack, three t-shirts, three pairs of underwear, three pairs of socks, jacket, fleece. Wash when you arrive at the day's destination and keep everything in your backpack. It's great to see how quickly I adapt to living in a dormitory and socializing with other people.

There are now four days left. The plan is to get to Burgos on Sunday, sleep there and then take the bus to Bilbao, see the city and then fly home on Tuesday.

Looking forward to the days here, so much happens every day when you walk for 4–5 hours, meet people at every café, different people in the evenings, live in different places, things that settle in, I cry, laugh, and become happier and calmer with each day. This is good for me. I'm happy that I'm here.

I began to listen more to my ability to pick up on other people's energies or moods. I noticed that I could suddenly become tired and feel a weight over my chest, and I wondered where it came from. When that change in my body came suddenly, I now began to ask questions. Who or what does this energy/mood belong to? Instead of acting immediately on a changed feeling in me, I asked why it had changed. I lifted up the feeling, like I was holding its hand, "Hello, feeling, where do you come from and to whom do you belong?" If I didn't do this, all these feelings became difficult to manage, and I suffered from a lot of brooding and emotional unrest. Now, I could learn to sort through and clear up any thoughts that arose.

I also felt how I began to change my values. Before I went on this trip, I was worried about what it would be like to live in hostels. Will people disturb me? Will they get annoyed if I go to the bathroom in the middle of the night? What if people stay up late and are noisy and I don't get to sleep? And so on. But wow—how quickly it can change if you let go of control and try something new! And then the wonderful simplicity of having everything I needed in my backpack. I took each day as it came, just went along and enjoyed every day. The simplicity in this gave me so much each day, so many encounters, so many feelings. I didn't know that so much could happen in a day, both inside me and through all the exterior experiences. If you stay more in the present, so much more happens. I saw more nuances and got close to people in a different way when I was not constantly running around out of breath. There is a lot of truth in that saying, "Let the journey be the destination."

Thursday, June 29, 2017

I've arrived in the next village, hiked around 22 km today. Just did some yoga, needed it after today's leg.

Started out with the Swedes I met yesterday, picked up on one woman's negative attitude, everything is difficult and wrong. So, I wanted to move away from them and increased my pace. Then I met a couple of Scots, lovely people who lived in Burgos and taught English, and now they were thinking of going to Hong Kong for a year. That encounter gave me some inspiration to deal with things.

Got the usual: coffee, juice, and bocadillo at the first café after about 7 km. Then I caught up with a guy with two strollers and three kids. I helped him up a long hill. He was from Argentina and talked a lot about how important the Camino was, how we modern people do so much out of greed, how we should do more for other people while also focusing on ourselves and our goals in life. Like he said, "I have to do my thing even if I have kids to care for. By doing that, I show them that it's important so that they learn to do the same." I helped him up the hill, then we stopped for a while, ate some fruit and then I walked on alone. That was an interesting encounter, not the kind of person I would normally walk up to, tattoos on his head, tall, and looking like a Latino mafia guy, nice prejudices I have ☺ Shouldn't judge a book by its cover…

Then we entered a village that was depressing. It was run down but still had a golf course, pool and nice houses—but the village center was almost empty and the woman working in the café there looked bored. Odd feeling about the village, a façade but no joy or energy.

Thinking about what the Argentinian guy said. It's all about relation-ships, encounters here and now. If you don't help anyone else, it's not worth it, i.e. helping others is meaningful. Take care of yourself, find your purpose, and help others.

A lot to process today, I'll have to digest it and let it fall into place.

The encounter with the Argentinian guy was very interesting. He and his wife planned to hike the entire Camino, 800 km, with four kids. When we got to the top of the hill, I met his wife and their youngest. The kids were between one and eight years old. He had some very interesting perspectives about walking our own way while also helping others. If we sacrifice ourselves for others and always do things for other people, then we show our children that that is the way to behave. If we stress around trying to drive them everywhere, join practices, be here, be there, then we show our children that we have to stress to get things done. But what if we could do both, and show them that we have things to do that matter to us? Our children need to understand that we adults need to do our own thing to feel well. That way, we show our children that it is important to know what you need to feel well and take time to yourself. I think that we live by the creed, "treat others as you would like to be treated yourself," but we sometimes forget to take care of ourselves first. In order to be there for other people, we need to have energy ourselves. At the same time, the Argentinian guy talked about how what we do should in some way help other people. And I agree. We have to find our purpose and do that which makes us feel good—while helping others.

The empty village became an example of how we can construct façades so that everything looks good from the outside. There were things in the village which made it look good, a golf course, a pool and so on. But the feeling was one of emptiness. This reminds me of our lives today. We get stuff, we look good, and we have everything we should have to feel good. But the feeling and the presence is lacking. The simplicity, the warmth, and the presence disappear. There were several other villages that we passed through which were more run down but the warmth in the people we met was completely different. They were proud of their village and of themselves. The inside was more important than the façade.

Friday, June 30, 2017

It's a little colder today, windy and a bit rainy. I've had to use my jacket and fleece, this morning it was 10 degrees Celsius and 16 during the day, a little cooler and nice hiking weather.

Slept poorly at the last hostel, even though it was a nice place. Had a good lunch, so hungry even that I had two lunches, first a paella and then a pasta Bolognese. Spent a lot of time with the group, Paul from Ireland; Joanne and Sandra from the US; Scott, Connor, and Mike, also from the US. Feels like we're a family now that follow each other, we walk at different paces, sometimes someone will walk a bit further, but we meet on the road at different cafés and usually at the day's destination.

When we arrive, I usually do a bit of yoga, today I cried again but from joy because I have such a great group of people to be around, they like me for who I am. After yoga, I took a shower and washed some clothes. Then I usually eat a light lunch and rest a while, I write and then go out for dinner at around 7 or 8. I go to bed at around 9:30 and wake up at around 6. Such are my days.

I meet a lot of different people on the road. Today I met a woman from Austria, a theology student who had just finished her dissertation about what you want to do with your life and your connection to God, about finding your own way and different things that hinder you. We had an interesting discussion, but it was also annoying how she always turned the discussion to her own things, always an example, "I had also…." It stole my energy and I realize that I do the same sometimes, it's connected to listening, letting things take time and letting people share their story without me taking over.

Today and yesterday were focused on the future, relationships, spending time with other people, caring about and doing what I believe in. Spending time with this group and really feeling close to them means a lot. It's a great feeling and I get a little emotional, probably will be an emotional last night too… ☺

Now, I'm going with Sandra to look at the cathedral and some hermit houses in a mountain.

A sense of security and closeness was created during the hike. We became a "Camino family" and we all showed respect towards each other and our need to do our own Camino, our own journey. We had each other, there was time to talk and socialize, but we were also given time to ourselves. I think that was a big thing; we didn't make demands on each other, but we were there for each other when it was needed. If I felt that I needed to be alone, I said so and the others said, "OK, see you later." And so, I walked a couple of hundred meters ahead or behind the rest. Because we were so open and clear about our needs, everything was made simple. If I chose to walk alone for a while, it didn't have anything to do with anybody else. That is, if I wanted to walk by myself it didn't mean that I disliked someone but simply that I needed to let things sink in and think alone for a little while.

This was such an obvious thing during the pilgrimage, and to me it was an important aspect to bring home to my everyday life. You don't have to feel that you must be with someone else because they want to talk, or that you have to be with the group all the time. It is okay to be away for a while and take time to yourself, and then you can get together again. Imagine if we could take some time during a party or a dinner, or during a workday, to walk away for a moment and just be alone if we needed it. It has nothing to do with not wanting to spend time with the others, we simply need a little time to ourselves.

Saturday, July 1, 2017

We hiked 28 km today, started just before 6 am and arrived at around 1:30 pm. My legs were a bit tired today, but it went well. Started out with Paul and then walked the majority of the distance with Andy from Australia.

Today we're staying at a small village called Agés, and tomorrow we have a 22 km hike to Burgos, which will be my last leg this time. I will then have walked 12 days and around 290 km. I'll stay the night in Burgos and then go to Bilbao, stay one day there and fly home on Tuesday.

Nice day today, pretty good pace with Andy. Talked to him about rela-
tionships, how the last time he hiked the Camino he met a Spanish woman
who became his partner. How that went and how he is now single again
and cool with that. It's all about taking it easy; he said that it takes two
years to get over a divorce, but we'll see.

Then we talked about being forward, i.e. showing what you want. The
difference between being desperate and being clear about what you want.
I sometimes think that I don't want to hurry and stress but that is not the
same thing as being clear and showing what you want. As long as I talk
calmly and plainly and show clearly what I mean. I think that's good, to
show what you want without stressing it.

That's all for now, going to spend some time with the group!

It was good to talk about the divorce and get to feel that my grief must be
allowed to take the time and space it needs. A divorce is a major change
and it takes time for the body to let it go. We are all different in that regard and we need different ways to handle it, but it is vital that we show
ourselves the respect to let it take time. At the same time, it is okay that
it is difficult, and there is no right or wrong when it comes to managing
it. For me, it took a long time. People sometimes asked me if I had met
anyone new, if I had begun to date, and many people gave me advice that
might have suited them but didn't suit me. I also sensed an anxiety in
other people and that they felt sorry for me because I was alone. But for
me, it was the right thing to do to heal my own wounds before meeting
someone new. I was in no hurry; it was okay for me to be alone. There
is a time for everything and now was the time for my grief to leave, and
it must be allowed to take time.

This process simultaneously gave me a sense of security and confidence in walking my own way. I learned to calmly and clearly show—to
myself and others—that this is the right direction for me. It is all about
letting go of the fear of rejection. As I have said, it was very important
for me in the past to fit in, I felt stress or desperation about being a part

of the group. It now became clear that by being more of myself, and confident in that, I was meeting people who liked me for who I am. We showed each other respect, we gave each other space, and we enjoyed each other's company.

Sunday, July 2, 2017

Just had a meeting with Tilde from the Netherlands, we met at a bridge here in Burgos, went for a coffee and talked for three hours. Fantastic, I'll have to process it all... I'll write more about it tomorrow. I have now hiked my last day, 22 km. Now, I'll spend the night in Burgos and take the bus to Bilbao tomorrow. That will give me time for summary and reflection. Now it's time to meet the group and spend the last night with them.

Monday, July 3, 2017

I'm now in Bilbao, took the bus from Burgos at 10 am and arrived two hours later. I'll fly home tomorrow. It'll be good to have one day for reflection. Yesterday was an incredible day, first a good hike, arrived at Burgos at 11.30 am, we got to the hostel at 12. Then we visited the cathedral, and later I went to get the bus ticket. On my way back, I sat down by a bridge. That's where I met Tilde. She also stopped there, with her bike, we said hello since we were both looking at a wedding couple having a photo shoot. Then we started talking, we went for a coffee and a walk by the river that runs through town.

We talked about everything; synchronicity, life, the meaning of it, challenges, letting go of your fears, things we learn on the way. It's difficult to remember everything but it was as if our talk were the sum of the whole week; I got to talk about the stuff I've been thinking about and I got her thoughts and input on it. Tilde is 43 years old, has worked as a teacher, and has been traveling through Spain in her camper for a while now. She quit her job to follow her intuition. We talked about doing your own thing.

*About just being, asking questions, having time for yourself, following your
own path and letting go of your fears. Following your gut feeling and not
letting your rational mind get in the way. It's the same thing with stress and
anxiety; just be calm and trust that it will be okay. If anyone has questions
and is worried, it's their uncertainty, their worry—I can be calm in myself.*

*I told her about my challenges, about the "party days"—the time in my
life that I'm ashamed of—but she understood and told me her story. I realize that it was all just based on the fear of not being good enough. It was
good to talk about it. Exciting and a great feeling, and I got lots of advice
about things that I'm going to check out. It was just great meeting her and
three hours went by quickly.*

*Later that night, the whole Camino crew went out for wine and tapas. I
talked with everybody and said my goodbyes. A lot of stuff can sink in and
settle during a fourteen-day trip. I have come to know a bunch of people,
listened to their different stories, I've come close to these people, I've been
myself, I've cried out of gratitude over having done this thing, cried about
the divorce and not having expressed my feelings, cried because I've come
to know my Camino family, cried because I'm happy and look forward to
whatever comes. What a journey!*

Fears—to think how much they limit us. It was interesting to hear Tilde
from the Netherlands talk about her goal to gradually let her fears go,
and I felt that I was doing the same thing. By being courageous enough
to take different steps, daring to stand out, we open so many doors and
embrace new experiences. The fears we have today—are they helping us
to protect ourselves from real dangers or are they actually limiting us?
What is the actual fear? Is it that you will fail, that people will laugh, that
you will lose control? The fear can be that primitive control that holds
you back or makes sure you don't do anything stupid to be excluded
from the group or get yourself killed. But are all fears necessary today?
Imagine if instead we could look at the fear with a bit of perspective, lift
it up to the light and say, "Okay, now I'm afraid, is that something I need

what a man "should" have at that age. And what does that mean exactly? What are we supposed to achieve in our lives? Are you living your life *for you* or like you think you *should* live to be happy?

Saturday, July 15, 2017

I now feel that I need to distance myself from C. She asked me if I could take Julie to Dalarna, I thought about it for a while but didn't feel like it and it was okay instead that I watched her a couple of days in the apartment. And it feels much better. Feels like things pop up, like how I always come through and act nice. But I should probably say no and do what I want.

I'm also thinking now that it's important that I'm clear with what I want. For example, I want to work with leadership, so I have to be clear about that and not apologize for what I want. Drive in the direction I want, remain calm, prioritize relationships while at the same time not let other people's limitations and fears stop me. Be an inspiration instead, be open, and show the possibilities.

It has now stopped raining, I'm in a café and will now go for a walk. Write you later!

For the longest time, I had a hard time saying no whenever someone asked something of me. In a way, "Yes" had been my default answer, because I wanted to help if I could. Even if I had other things on my table, I tried to solve it. But to now begin to say no and feel that it is a yes to me and my own time—that was huge. For me, it had been shameful to choose myself, it was somehow egotistical. But what if a no to somebody is really a sign of respect towards myself and what I need right now? A no can lead to something else. The person might ask again if it is really important, and I can reconsider, but at least we now have a dialogue. If I say yes right away even though I don't want to, it is unkind both to me and to the person asking, because she or he doesn't know that I do it reluctantly. And it doesn't give me the right to be angry afterwards, because I said yes.

Saturday, July 15, 2017, continued

Have gone for a walk in a lull between the rains, and then had lunch. Got a message from C, a picture of Julie and the text, "Because of the divorce, I need to get rid of Julie." That made me upset, felt like it was my fault, but maybe it's just C's way of quickly getting someone to take the dog off her hands. But it struck a nerve anyway, and even if it's decided, it's going to be tough. My focus now will be on the kids, see how they're doing and how tough it is for them with the Julie situation.

I think I need more time, get some distance, and make sure to have fun before I start working again. I will take three more weeks off, and then get back to business. I'll continue to have this relaxed feeling. Take time to do things, walk, exercise, do yoga, read, swim, and enjoy all of it. Meet friends and have fun, be calm in myself.

Just think about how I've felt of such little worth. Like my thoughts and feelings were wrong, that I didn't bring up my feelings or ruminations out of fear that C would get angry and that I might lose her and the kids. And see how that went...

There will be more disagreements now that I choose to walk my own way, but things will work out because I mean well. And we just have to talk about it, I will express my feeling and be humble towards others. I'm not afraid of being wrong, I gladly accept advice from others, I'm here to learn.

It's tough about Julie, that she's going to be given away, but I don't really spend that much time with her. The days I had her were fun but also limiting. I think it's going to be good for her to come to a family where they have time for her. I'll cherish these last days with her and have fun. I also realize that this is connected to our separation. When Julie isn't around anymore, it won't come as naturally for me and C to see each other.

I wish C all the luck in the world on her journey ahead, hope she'll be well and reach her own insights. I'll be here and I'll help when the feeling is right, but I also realize that it's her own journey. I won't solve her problems for her. I'm now letting go of Julie with sadness and tears, but it'll be alright. I'm now letting go of my fear of not being good enough for C. My feeling is the uncomfortable feeling trigger memories and emotional responses in you, making you want to either run away or roll up your sleeves and solve the problem (flight or fight). But remember that this particular situation is not about you, and that you just need to be there for the other person. It is often enough, in my experience, that we are present, giving them time to put their thoughts into words. We can help them simply by listening and being there with our presence and warmth, thereby creating a safe space in which our friend can be vulnerable. If we look to ourselves, this is most often what we need when we are having a tough time; to talk about it, to be sad, to just *be*. At least, that is the case for me. What if we can make it easier to help each other by simply being there?

Saturday, August 19, 2017

Sitting on a mountain top by Oxsjön looking out across the lake. I'm on a hike, stopped halfway for a break, hiking 10 km in total. It's been an interesting first week, if you can call it a first week, but it feels a bit like it as it is the week when everyone is back at work after the summer vacation. It has been up and down; as I wrote, Monday was confusing but then quiet.

Tuesday went by fine, good meeting with the potential client. Right, I also visited my ex-father-in-law and his partner. I appreciate talking to her, she is a warm and caring person. She said something that I will carry with me, and it was to share my thoughts and be the open and caring person that I am also in my work. Dare to be myself and show it, I don't have to play any roles. It felt good and I will take that with me.

The housing situation is good too, I think we need each other right now. My landlord is happy that I'm there and she is on her own journey. And for me it's also good, nice to have someone else in the apartment, get to hear her thoughts and reflect on them. Let her talk and I only need to give it time and listen. Sometimes I can feel a bit stressed there though, but I realize that I just have to listen and take it easy. And be clear if I want to leave or do something else.

Mm, it feels good anyway and fun, it's going to be an exciting and interesting fall. Going on a yoga retreat next weekend, that'll be fun too!

It was interesting to hear that I should bring more of myself into my work. I realized that I entered a work role and acted a certain way because it was expected. But really—as an independent consultant I create my own brand and it is me. By being more of me in my work, I get to work with and get hired by people who appreciate me for who I am. But I had brought my old role from the last company, and it carried with it a certain behavior in client meetings. I needed to find a new way of thinking and letting the new thoughts shape themselves. This is also connected to the saying, "The journey is the destination." If I adapt too much to get a certain assignment at a client, I have to play that role during the whole project. That means I have to give in, and things may get tense. My ex-father-in-law's partner has been an independent consultant for many years, and it was good to get her input. What I create now with myself as brand is long-term. By sharing more of myself, I will get more assignments where I am appreciated and where I appreciate being.

Monday, August 21, 2017

Yesterday I took the kids to a movie and before that I met some friends, had a really good day. Then something weird happened. I gave the boys a ride home to C and went in to say goodbye but then I felt I couldn't stay. I went out to the car and was sad, then when I got home I felt like going for a walk because I had so many emotions to sift through. It felt strange, I thought I was over C, but something popped up and made me sad. Maybe there is still a hope that we might have something. So, when I came home, I talked with my landlord and she made me realize that if I think we still have something, then I should tell C.

So, I called C today and mentioned that I miss her and wanted to tell her that maybe there is something between us after all. As a final thought now that she wants to start dating. And I get a little insecure when she wants to see me, feels like she sometimes wants more but isn't saying it. So, I thought I should say it straight out. But she was clear about not wanting, she doesn't feel anything like that, she wants to get out there and meet new people and has put me in the "friend department." And of course, she says that if it's difficult for me we shouldn't see each other, and I think it's time. She gets to do her thing and I will see the boys when it works out and we'll have fun together. But I'm still happy I brought it up. Sure, I could've said it later if we had seen each other some more, but it would've been tough to have it on my mind and nurture that small hope. I will put that and the separation behind me.

Time to look ahead! Step by step, day by day, finding new goals and a vision, that's what I'll do.

I was happy that I had the courage to be open about my feelings with C. I got a feeling, a thought, and I began to think about different scenarios, painting different pictures of how things could be. In the past, I brooded over such things for long periods of time, but now I was getting faster and faster at acting and expressing what I felt. By having the courage to express how I felt and being confident about it, I avoided all this brooding. I had taken ownership of my wellbeing—by allowing myself to be vulnerable and talking about feelings, I could talk about the things that otherwise would have tormented me, and it made me feel free. At the same time, I didn't put any demands or expectations on C; I just said it in a simple way. At the base of it all, it is about being honest towards yourself and others.

CHAPTER 11

Honest Towards Myself and Others

Thursday, August 24, 2017

Back on my bench in Österlen ☺ Arrived at the yoga retreat yesterday, and it's now early morning. Excited to see what will happen this time. Since yesterday evening, my thoughts revolve around what I want to do. It feels like my whole body is bubbling and I want to do stuff, but I don't know what. I also feel impatient for something to happen and I want things to do. Mm, what do I want to accomplish? What would I be proud to succeed with? Yes, I'm back a little in my old routines, even though I do have my own business now. But what are my goals, what do I want to accomplish? What is my purpose? What makes me feel good? How do I reach out?

It's also a bit scary to state your goals, I think, because what happens if you fail? But it's also hard to not know. But do I need goals? One goal can be to feel well. Maybe that's where I am right now. Mm, no matter what, I have some interesting days ahead ☺

A lot was happening at the same time and I felt a kind of ambivalence, like I was stepping on the gas and the brake simultaneously, or perhaps driving forward without a map. I had been through many big changes during the past six months. The separation was finally settling in with me, but then I had to deal with the new job and looking for a new apartment again. Somehow, I felt that I needed to know where I was headed. If someone asked me what I wanted, I didn't know right then, and it was hard to not know what my goal was. And even if I had known what the goal was, what if I failed? Many thoughts were spinning around inside my head—but I guess that is natural in a situation like this. I had to find my calm somehow and allow myself to be in that uncomfortable feeling, and also feel some kind of faith that things would work out eventually. At the same time, I didn't need to have all the answers about what I would accomplish. I didn't know yet and that was okay. I almost felt a certain calmness about not knowing; I was more worried about what I would tell others who asked me. There was a self-imposed expectation that I should know what to say when someone asked me.

Friday, August 25, 2017

Day two at the retreat and this morning we were woken up at 5 o'clock, and then we went down to Haväng to do yoga at sunrise. Felt great after a while, but I was stiff to begin with. Been a bit sad too and I could now let go a little more of C, need to let go to move on.

A lot was spinning in my head yesterday, finding my plan going forward, what I should do about housing, work, travels, etc. A lot of different thoughts were flying all over the place. My body hurt when we did yoga, especially my back and I felt we were sitting too much. My head also hurt, guess from lack of coffee... And I thought: How will this weekend work out, will I make it through it?

We talked a lot about greatness, being yourself, we repeated the steps to change with admitting, locating, and releasing the old and finding a new intention and acting on it. Things were bubbling up in me and I feel that I'm in the worry phase, taking small steps and choosing that which makes me feel good, travels, new job, peace and quiet.

I'm grateful for our relationship, mine and C's, how I have been brave enough to challenge myself more and had C to support me on my journey in a humble and understanding way. She has challenged me and helped me grow whenever I stopped myself, "Going to the bathroom on a boat." With the kids, changing my diet, starting to do yoga. Then her choices at the end, with her stuff, made me see how much I have done for us, and my burnout made me pause and really think about relationships and work. I chose to pause, listen to my highly sensitive personality and go deep within myself. It was incredibly important that I did, because my old memories and behaviors were lodged so deep inside.

I am grateful for the challenges I have been through, because they have helped me grow as a person. I have developed and learned much about myself in my relationship with C. I am even grateful that I was burned out! My confidence has grown, and I have discovered more and more of the things I have censured from myself. That is why I am both sad about the separation and happy that C has been there, sharing my journey. My philosophy is that the challenges and resistance you face on your life's journey are teachers. It is all about learning more about yourself when you face a challenge. For in the end, the way you feel is mostly in your head. We live and experience the world in our own brain and in our own universe. What if your wellbeing doesn't have anything to do with anyone else, but only with your own experience and how you deal with your feelings and thoughts?

Sunday, August 27, 2017

I feel very calm this morning, feel that all this about right and wrong is gone. I mean, all that thinking about whether I'm making the right deci-sion about everyday things, housing, work, and what I should do to make it right in the future. I've come "down from my head" and feel more in my body, light or heavy. Also moving down in my speech, talking from my stomach, have thought about it before but it now feels calmer and in place. I let my shoulders down, relax, open my chest, and have the courage to take up space. There are so many words, but if I now challenge myself and feel a difference, then I know that my body has received it.

Yesterday we talked about "No"—what does it mean, what value is there in a no, etc. Realize that I've taken a no personally, but it's not personal. How I can feel like I'm in the way if I ask something of someone, and how a no really is an honest answer from the other person and a yes to them-selves. Also, that a no can trigger energy and that I need to explain further if they don't understand.

Then we did an exercise down in Kivik, we had to go around and ask questions to unknown people and make sure we got a no for an answer. I thought it was really difficult, but challenged myself and asked a few questions, like if they had sugar free wares or something else in the grocery store. Then I felt that it isn't so bad to get a no. I also realize that I have been bad at saying no, but a no to someone can be a yes to myself. Great insight, it makes everything much calmer.

This thing about getting a no gave me new perspectives. It is connected to having the courage to ask, otherwise you don't know what the answer is. In the past, I added value to it and took it personally when someone said no. But what if it isn't so bad, what if it is okay? It is okay that someone says no because they don't want to; it has nothing to do with you. Perhaps it is a bad time, they have other plans, the woman has a boyfriend, or the client doesn't need your help at the moment. If I ask, I will get an answer and that will help me decide how to move on. If I want to create or get jobs, and meet a woman in the future, I must ask and be prepared for a no. It is inevitable and a necessary step in moving on.

Monday, August 28, 2017

Back in Gothenburg again. What a great extended weekend in Österlen, and what new insights! The last day, yesterday, was so good, felt relaxed and secure. It's amazing how much it can give and how much things can sink in in only four days.

My landlord just got home, and it's working out just fine to be room-mates. One thing I'm unaccustomed to is all the talking, sometimes I feel like she has a need to constantly talk and I'm being kind and listening. In reality, I feel many things: on the one hand, it works well when we talk but on the other hand, it feels like she has to talk when we are both in the same room. So, I'll have to practice listening and tell her when I want some me-time. I mean, I appreciate silence. Then I realize that I might have acted the same way, that I have kept talking and bringing up things to fill a void. And that can be somewhat annoying, I realize that now. C mentioned it several times.

Wow, just got a bit of news, C has met a man... and she wants me to know that she's told the kids and their father, and that they are switching weeks because he, the new man, also has custody of his kids every other week, and they're doing it to sync.

My reaction... relief, a little surprised somehow. A light feeling, no anger, sadness, or anything, I guess I knew this was coming somehow, and then I'm in a calm state of mind since the yoga retreat. Guess they've been seeing each other for a while, which means there was surely something she didn't tell me the last time I saw her. But it doesn't matter, I don't want to spend any more energy on that. Well, that's the extra piece of news today.

Now it's time for a tired Thomas to go to bed. Right, I realized that it was good to talk to my landlord when I got the news, so that's fine ☺

I gain perspective of myself regarding silence. In the past, I felt that I should speak when someone else was close by, but I now felt an increasing appreciation for silence—being silent enables you to reflect. I now practiced saying that I wanted to be alone even though we were only two people in the room. It was great that my landlord and I had such a good dialogue that we could practice this and laugh at how we tried and behaved. In the past, I thought that people saw me as a boring person if I was silent, and that I was rude if I didn't listen. But such a situation involves two people with different perspectives, and you don't always have to talk or listen. It is okay to say, "I'm thinking about something right now and I'd appreciate it if we didn't talk."

It can also have to do with the fact that many people find it difficult to be "in their own company" and are afraid of this. You would rather talk to someone else and fill the silence than go into yourself, because that is scary. I have read a study in which they put people alone in a room. The only thing to do was to press a button which would give you a small electric shock, an uncomfortable sensation. But most people would rather press the button than be alone with their thoughts! I recognize this from my previous behavior; I wanted to book up my evenings and weekends with friends and acquaintances because I found it difficult to be alone. But that changed, and I now felt, more and more, that it was okay to be alone with my own thoughts.

Thursday, August 31, 2017

Yesterday I had a fun meeting; through Lovisa I've made contact with a person who might be able to rent out an apartment. I went there to have a look but ended up staying for over two hours. We had a lot in common, hiking, yoga, both have studied in Linköping, worked in the same student pub. And she lives in Italy now and had many interesting perspectives on differences between Sweden and Italy. Encounters like this are so much fun and it's great to just talk spontaneously like that. I realize that my calm and my confidence enable me to open up and share much—and it makes everything so much easier. And she gave me some good ideas. In Italy, it is people first and work second, but in Sweden, it's the other way around. They are more open about feelings and talk more openly. Interesting perspectives and she gave me feedback on how she appreciated my openness and the way I was connected to my emotions. I think I'll get the apartment, would be great, a one-year lease from October. Regardless, it was an interesting encounter that I will take with me.

One thing the woman with the new apartment told me was that she was an engineer like me. In Sweden, engineers are seen as possible CEOs and appreciated as leaders. But when she mentioned her profession in Italy, she felt that the people there thought, "But who will we then discuss philosophy with, and history, and life?" In Italy, engineers are seen as builders, not as thinkers. That was interesting for me to hear, as I have felt that my contemplativeness and sensitivity have not sat well with the engineering companies I have worked for.

It was also interesting to hear how work comes first in Sweden. And it is true. In Sweden, the first question people ask you, after they ask your name, is, "What do you do for a living?" My new landlord (yes, I got the apartment) told me that in Italy, she has known people for years and known a lot about them—but not their occupation. It is somehow not interesting; the important thing is who you are as a person. You also ask more questions there; you are interested in other people in a different way. She describes it as a genuine curiosity about the person you are talking to.

In my experience, we Swedes, or at least the people where I have worked, find it difficult to deal with feelings and emotions. We are unaccustomed to it and become afraid when feelings come up. We almost see it as something wrong when someone acts on a feeling or is being emotional. We like the façade where everything is in order, and we should leave our emotions and feelings at home. There are of course different perspectives on this, but I feel that we miss out on some of life's true content if we aren't allowed to be the sensitive creatures we were made to be. Not only do we miss out on a richer life experience, but there is also one particular danger with not allowing ourselves to be emotional. What we miss is that our emotions are natural signals that can guide us in different situations. If we constantly block our emotions, we will hinder ourselves and might go against ourselves, making decisions that are not good for us. If we look again at the Swedish work environment, where we are encouraged to leave emotions at home—what kind of decisions do we make in our day-to-day work? I think that my burnout answers that question. This does not, however, mean that we should always air our thoughts and feelings, but we should learn to understand the reason behind them, learn to listen to them and understand their message, and be able to discuss them if and when we need to.

Sunday, September 3, 2017

Sunday afternoon, home again after the day's activities. Up early, went for a walk, and after breakfast I got ready to go over to the kids. Then I started to think about C and her new man. Wonder who it is? Does it matter? Should I spend any more energy there? No, I shouldn't, she must be allowed to make her own decisions, but it still affects me, maybe that's not so strange... Anyway, it was a fun day with the kids, went to a soccer game, and afterwards we all went and had ice cream close to my place.

Sent a text to C just now wishing her good luck, feels good, now I'll close that.

So glad that I've taken time to reflect, that I quit my job, got the time to pause, that I've had my own business since mid-May, had time to myself, let things sink in. That I've been able to let go of the old stuff with relationships and work. That I've gone to yoga retreats and allowed everything to settle, reflected, met wonderful people (okay, pause for happy tears). So glad that I will now face life with this liberating sense of confidence in being myself.

It had, as you can see, been a little back and forth with C and my feelings for her. I was proud that I brought up my feelings and told C about them. I also allowed myself to grieve and be sad when needed. I listened to my body and my own emotional management, brought up and scrutinized different perspectives. I took responsibility for my own grieving process and emerged stronger. It was now about six months since I moved out of the house and seven months since we decided to get a divorce. I felt no animosity or anger towards C for having met a new man. As my therapist told me in January, I can only influence my own choices and thoughts. I cannot influence the other person except by expressing how I feel. So, it felt good to be able to move on and also know that she had chosen to move on. Now, I felt that there were no more doubts about whether we might get back together.

Thursday, September 7, 2017

On Tuesday night, I got an okay on the apartment in Linné, feels great, moving in in October. I can now let go of the apartment search for a while, the lease is a full year. It's fun to sublet, it creates dynamics and generates new encounters.

I have talked a lot with my current landlord these last couple of days. She is going through a lot right now. Moving things out of her ex's apartment and leaving a lot of emotional stuff there. At the same time, she talks a lot and shares things that she needs to let go of. A difficult childhood, very bad things that come up. I was somewhat prepared for it but it's heavy and I'm glad that she opens up and talks about it. She's on a difficult journey and she's very strong. It was a fortunate thing that we became roommates. But such a heavy thing she's going through and the stuff we're talking about at home, it's like therapy... And I get to talk a lot too, and it's great to have someone to talk to.

Yes, it's weird, but I guess it takes time before all the new stuff sinks in and becomes normal. Sometimes I wonder if I'm turning into an oddball because I spend so much time alone, thinking and doing my stuff. But now that I'm writing it, it's not that big a difference from before. Then, I used to sit among people but still alone. The only difference now is that I'm not in an office.

I'm also thinking about what I will do in the future. I want to use my feelings in some way. Talk with people on a deeper level, be there for them, and help them.

I continued to see how my landlord opened up and how I contributed simply by being there for her and creating a safe space. She opened up about many painful memories which had affected her for many, many years. I had experience from cleaning out old memories through my journey and the different retreats, and I recognized the process in her. I was there for her and I asked questions to help her locate the basis for her pain. We peeled that onion, going through the emotional layers and the things lodged in her body. She shined a new light on how she had been affected by painful things that happened in her childhood, how she had felt responsible and ashamed of certain events that had affected her ever since. With this understanding, she gained a new perspective of the choices she had made throughout her life. How the limitations from her childhood had kept her from believing and letting people into her life. She was incredibly strong in her journey and she understood and forgave herself step by step. We eventually got to the choices she made today, and she recognized how she sometimes chased affirmation and was blind to her own worth. She learned to let go of her old limitations and open up for the things she wanted to do, instead of fighting or bending over backwards to fit in. It was amazing to see her inner strength, how she grew and gained confidence.

Looking at my own experiences, and what I have gleaned of other people's experiences, it is interesting to note how much of our behavior is a result of things that happened in our childhood. What I did here with my landlord was that we "talked" to the little girl she was when she was a child. Together, we made her understand that it wasn't her fault. We found more and more events that she could let go of in light of her adult self. Because she could see these events in a new light, she could see herself differently. She could see that she is worth much more, she doesn't have to adapt for people to like her, she is invaluable as she is. I am glad that I got to be there with her and guide her through the process and see the relief on her face. To me, that is making a difference in a person's life.

CHAPTER 12

Letting Go

Tuesday, September 12, 2017

I have now booked my trip to Australia, feels so damned good that it'll happen!!! Leaving on December 20 and coming home on January 12. This weekend, I felt that now is the time to go, talked to my friends who live outside Perth, and it suited them. So now I will finally do it, I have longed for this trip and now it's happening!! ☺ This is my 40th birthday gift to myself.

I was now following my feelings. For many years, I had wanted to go to Australia, but it never happened. I thought about what kind of feeling I would like to have in March the following year. Would I regret it if I didn't go? A clear yes to that. So, I might as well book the tickets. I began by checking where to stay and then booked the tickets—the rest would work itself out, I knew it would. The important thing was to get going.

Sunday, September 17, 2017

What a couple of days. Just got back after a taking the kids to a jazz concert, really fun. And before that I went to a lecture called "Turn Work into Yoga" with Jonas Freeman, a Swedish guy who lives in Bali. Thoughts about stress and how you find your calm at work, i.e. bring a yoga feeling into work. Anyway, it was so much fun with the concert, glad I brought the boys and that they liked it very much.

Such great and exciting days now, loving it and how does it get any better than this? ☺ *Happy about the lecture today, I met some new people that I will meet again later in connection to a discussion club about HSP. New ideas about what I will do and how I will share my experiences. Life coach perhaps? Lecturer? Write a book?*

Many good ideas and thoughts popped up during the *Turn Work into Yoga* lecture, i.e. how to bring the calm from the yoga mat to work. Why are we stressed in certain situations and not in others? Why do we stress at work while we can create things in a calm state of mind at home? At home, we can do many things, and we can (usually) do them without stress; we can create with joy and calm. But why is it so much work to work? What are we stressed about? If you are getting chased by a tiger, then the stress is good for you as it helps you escape the situation and survive. But we don't have that kind of stress at work, it isn't about survival and running from a dangerous animal. It is about deadlines, processes, and work procedures that are invented by us. It is not a matter of life and death, but we sometimes stress as if it were. The tricky thing about stress is that it spreads as we pass our emotions onto other people. I remember one of the most important tasks I had as a project manager. It was to not spread the stress from the steering group or their anxiety about the progress of the project to the project group. I had to be a filter, because if that stress spread, everybody would run around like headless chicken doing a lot of things they needn't do.

So, the question is how we can bring more calm into the things we do at work. How do you transfer the balance from the yoga mat, or from other situations where you create in a calm state of mind, to work? How do you filter and sort your thoughts and feelings to create without stress?

Wednesday, September 20, 2017

I'm now in my "other office," the café Da Matteo. Today I'm a bit tired and worn out, slept poorly but also realizing that it has been a lot these last few days. Lots of new people and many events over the last couple of days. Lots of new contacts and much listening. And tonight, I'm going to see "The Phantom of the Opera" with Joakim, that'll be fun! But it's also good to have a free weekend, I'll take it easy and just relax.

I have a lot of new and different contacts and it takes more energy than I think sometimes. It feels right and it is fun, but it's the balance I'm after. I'm happy for all that's happening, many fun encounters, new thoughts, new inspiration, and that I'm calm and myself in these new encounters. Good that I'm landing my first job soon, it's going to be great to get started, participate and create something, and all the while giving me the opportunity to invest in new things. I plan to take a mindfulness class and maybe a yoga instructor class or an HSP life coaching course. See what that can bring. I'm thinking something with HSP and coaching, and helping to prevent burnout, especially for people like me. Increase understanding among highly sensitive persons and those who are close to highly sensitive persons.

Sunday, September 24, 2017

Today I feel a bit low… Yesterday I talked to my roommate and we started talking about what it can be like to live with someone who is burned out, and I came to think of me and C. How it was during the years I didn't feel well, or rather, now that I'm writing about it, how we both had a lot to deal with then. Thinking about whether I should say something or send info about what it means to be in a relationship with someone who has suffered from burnout.

The tricky thing is that I didn't understand myself that I was down, and she didn't understand either. I began to realize it around the time we filed for divorce, and I mentioned it then, but it was already too late. Is there anything I could have done differently, is it my highly sensitive self that wants to correct things? Or am I just sad? It's a pity I didn't realize before that I wasn't well and that it wasn't easy to be around me. Too bad it went as far as a divorce. I should probably bring it up with her sometime…

It wasn't until now that I admitted to myself that I had been ill, suffering from burnout, or exhaustion syndrome. Earlier, I had only said that I had something akin to it. That I was stressed, I had a lot to deal with, but I didn't really think that I was ill. And I was never on sick leave or looked for any support or aid. But the more I read about and understand what a burnout entails for yourself and the people around you, the more everything clicked into place. It was very difficult for me to admit that I had been ill. I shouldn't get ill, that wasn't me, I was a person who helped other people.

There were many signals and I have mentioned them earlier in my story. I would now like to directly address those of you who do things for everyone else and who feel stressed. Read up on burnout/exhaustion syndrome. Pause and think about whether that fits the description of you. Catch the signals early. Begin to talk and admit to yourself that it is okay, even if you feel it is difficult. It is okay to ask for help. I speak for myself, who caught it relatively early, but I know of many people who have suffered far worse. If you get really ill it will take a very long time to recover, so think about what causes the stress you feel. Is it a tiger chasing you or do you create your own stress?

Wednesday, September 27, 2017

I'm at a café in Lindholmen. Began the day with a little yoga at home as usual. Then I went to a networking meeting and then had lunch with a friend who is about to start a business in the gym sector. Good day so far, feeling less tired today, got to bed early last night. I hope my cold is going away. I have a slight headache and have been tired in general these last few days, perhaps one reason why I've felt a bit low. Felt alert and calm in the meetings I've had today. Now I'm waiting for an answer about my first assignment.

It's very exciting to have so much time. A lot of thought about what one wants to do, how one manages time when there are no musts. How sweet it can be to have things to do, because then you don't think about what you want to do and what should be done. You don't think about how often/seldom you meet friends or talk to them. If you have a family with a wife and kids, time flies and if you hang out with friends a couple of time per month, that's a lot. Now that I'm alone, there's more time, but my friends have lots of other things to do and are in another phase. How to deal with that and what do I do with my time? I'm glad that I have a roommate now, because I've had someone to spend time with in a simple way. How will it be in the future? When I live alone again, have jobs, and spend time at my clients'.

Mm, interesting, and today I'm going to the house to see C and the boys. Haven't really spoken to her since we met at Eriksberg in mid-August, before she told me she had met a new man.

It was such a big difference after the separation; all of a sudden, I had a lot of time to myself. If you have experienced a separation, maybe you can identify with this. You now have the children every other week or, like me, only sporadically. You want to fill the "empty" week and you might feel lonely and friendless. It is a weird situation, as your friends are there but they might be too busy with their families, just like you used to be. And you may now have other expectations about how often you can and want to meet your friends. Earlier, you had a natural social network through your family and the children's activities since everybody was in the same phase. It might also seem like it was easier to have a family and everything that goes with it, because you always had something to do and you weren't "forced" to think about what you wanted to do; you didn't have to be alone with yourself. It can be difficult to spend so much time with yourself because you are not used to it. At this point, you have to be kind to yourself, let the change settle in and slowly but steadily test your ground and discover what you want to fill your time with.

Monday, October 2, 2017

I'm sitting on the couch in my apartment, it's been a fun and intense day. Been at the new apartment to check on things, talked, and fixed a few things. Feels great to move there, and strange at the same time. Subletting again. I'm getting rid of my stuff because the new apartment comes furnished. Everything's up and down and still it feels fantastic.

Also had a coaching session with the guy who held the "Turn Work into Yoga" workshop a couple of weeks ago. It gave me a sense of calm in continuing in the direction I'm headed, and I will keep doing things that feel good. Right, I was at the book fair again on Sunday and thought about how many lovely people I met and saw. As if I opened my eyes and truly saw how many great people there are and how much I've struggled to fit in in different places. An incredible sensation and also a sadness over not having realized this until now. But mostly a positive sensation, I think.

It also felt great when I went to the archipelago for a long walk on Amund Island on Saturday, and I felt so happy and alive. So simple and yet so great. We talked about that during the coaching session, that something can be very simple and yet very good. I'm now going to continue doing the things that make me feel good, sharing, and being there for others, and we'll see where it takes me.

At this time, I appreciated the simplicity in being alone, but also the warmth when I met new people in new contexts. In the past, I thought a lot about what I should do, that there had to be some activity for me to go to. Now, I appreciated just going out for a long walk. Nothing had to happen, I felt good just going out. In the past, I also thought a lot about daily planning, what I should do, and then nothing came of it. Now, I kept it simple there too. I didn't know what the day would bring, but starting it with a walk sounded good and then I would simply see what happened. Once I was out and moving, I would think of the next thing to do or figure out what I felt like. An expression I began to use privately was "get moving." I didn't know what would happen, but to get moving was the crucial thing. To start and move my body. Go for a walk to let my thoughts settle and give birth to new ideas. Go to a fair or some other new thing. I didn't need to know exactly what it would bring; the important thing was to go. Might it bring new encounters? New inspiration? Or perhaps nothing that time, but then I would know.

Tuesday, October 10, 2017

Sitting in my new apartment in Linné. Moved the last of my stuff on Sunday and have now stayed here two nights. I've cleaned out the old apartment, packed up, and got rid of stuff. Gave away the dresser and armchair, sold my outdoor furniture, I'm giving away the bed. So, the only furniture I brought with me were two nightstands, four kitchen chairs, and Grandpa's old wooden chair. Otherwise only clothes, books, kitchen utensils, and other small stuff. Feels great to get rid of things. It was a bit tough too, the move, guess it stirred up emotions from the last time I moved, so I felt a bit low, especially on Saturday. Then, when I found my wedding ring, I broke down and cried. But it felt good afterwards and it wasn't really that I miss her, it was more that I was reminded, I think.

It's really new on all fronts right now and it's great that the lease is for a year, at least. And workwise, I'll soon start my first job. So good to have a first assignment there so that I can land a little when it comes to work too. I got the name and phone number of a woman that a friend thought would be a good match for me, but I realize that I'm not ready to date yet. It wouldn't be fair to either of us, because I'm not ready to commit right now. At least, that's how it feels. I'd love to meet the people I've gotten to know naturally, but to contact someone with the expectation of dating is too much right now. And that's okay ☺

That's all for now!

When I moved from the house, I saved a lot of stuff and rented a storage unit. I got rid of a lot then too, but there was also a lot left. During the six months that passed before I moved again, I didn't miss a single object in that storage unit. Now, I knew that I would sublet for at least a year and the apartment was already furnished. So why should I keep my furniture? It only took up space. I didn't know where I would live later on or what that place would look like, so there wasn't much use in keeping it all. It was an incredible relief to get rid of more stuff. What is it that we cling to? I used to cling to many things in that storage unit ("This one and that might be good to keep") but the storage unit became full. Sure, it might be smart to keep a few things, but I think it is important that we don't cling to material objects. I also noticed how clearing out the storage unit stirred up many emotions. It really hurt and I got sad when I found the wedding ring. Perhaps that is a reason why we cling to things, old memories and such that make it difficult to throw things out. I also think of that which we may call the emotional backpack, all those feelings and emotions we carry with us because it is difficult to sort through them. But somewhere along the road we must get rid of stuff, both material objects and feelings, because it gets very heavy to carry it all.

Monday, October 16, 2017

A quiet evening: after trombone class with J, I went home and went for a run in Änggården. Felt I needed some fresh air and it was a fine evening. Ran 10 km and when I got home, I did some yoga. Felt great and I feel that my fatigue from yesterday has turned into a sense of calm.

Feels great to land in all the new now, to have my new place, good to have a place of my own, a base, and to find my calm. I almost can't believe how much has happened lately! So many new contacts, my former and current landlords, new networks, all the old contacts, colleagues and friends I've had lunch with, and the El Camino family, what a year and so many new things that must settle in my head and my body. Deeper relationships with the kids and their father, with Mom and her partner, Dad and my brother. My wonderful friends through the yoga retreats. Got a little emotional and had to take a break, so grateful and happy that I'm being appreciated for who I am. So many encounters with people and I have truly been myself. Relationships have grown deeper, I feel better (emotional to just write about it… ☺ *) Wow… how does it get even better than this?* ☺

I now experienced the benefits of pausing and feeling gratitude. At the end of my morning meditation, I tried to recognize the things which I was grateful for that day. Showing gratitude is inherent in many religions, and several studies show that we feel better when we express gratitude. I can always tell a difference when I do this exercise; I am happier and things around me become clearer somehow. One important thing for me is that I am actually healed now, I have a clear mind, I can move freely. I can think. I have friends around me. I can see these things more clearly and can then value them a little higher. In my experience, many of us forget that which we have closest around us, we take it for granted. I know I have, and it isn't perhaps until we lose something that we truly recognize what we had. Reflecting upon the things you are happy and grateful about in your life can make you express it before it is too late, and this is important.

Even if we are relatively healthy both physically and mentally, we tend to create problems for ourselves and make things more difficult than they are. But we are all strong, and we have the ability to move on. It has to do with confidence and courage. A friend of mine is a role model when it comes to trying to look to the future. He was diagnosed with a severe form of cancer in the stomach and brain and fought it for three years. He was then declared cancer free and is now looking at a period of recovery that will naturally take a lot of energy. At the same time, he values every day, especially considering the fact that the doctors told him four times during the treatment that he should have died. He now rejoices over simple acts like going down to the grocery store or just going out the door. Step by step, he is moving on and he is always positive and grateful for all the assistance from people around him.

A lot happens to us in life and we all have our own personal challenges. All the while, we already have a lot around us that we may value and rejoice over. What are you grateful for?

CHAPTER 13

Standing Up for Yourself

Thursday, October 26, 2017

The lecture on Tuesday was great, a good group of people and interesting discussions. In the evening, I met up with Eric, who is visiting Gothenburg. I was a bit tired on Wednesday and it was a heavy day, but still good. Some trouble with my old employer and my new assignment. But before that, I talked to my coach Jonas and got to resolve some old stuff, my values regarding my old employer. And how I get difficult when I'm communicating with them, and that's exactly how I don't want to be. So, he helped me let go of it, the anxiety over that it won't work out, I've had that feeling a long time, what will happen, all the trouble, etc. So, I talked with them and told them all about it. I have been contacted about an assignment, what's your view of it? We'll see what happens, and it feels good, great to let it go.

I ended up in a dilemma with my old employer. We didn't see eye to eye about whether the assignment I might get violated an old deal and how to move forward. In this case, my coach was very supportive. I was open with how I felt and thought, and he helped me and guided me through my emotions. The situation stirred up old memories and I fell back into a pattern and a behavior I didn't want. He helped me see what was happening and thanks to that, I could change my attitude. It is important to be honest with how you feel, and by putting your feelings into words and sharing them with others, you gain perspective. It is easy to blame others and say they are being difficult, but I was becoming difficult too. I am responsible for my behavior and for how I want things to be.

Tuesday, October 31, 2017

Went for a run this morning, felt so great, needed it. There's been so much else going on these last few days and I've missed my calm. Talked to my old employer yesterday, felt a little tense and I realize I make things difficult. Felt that a lot of old stuff popped up, which I haven't told them before. There is frustration and irritation there, which I began to let go of today. Great to let go of old stuff in that context too. I realize that it has to do with me not expressing how I feel for too long, and it's good to vent it.

It is as if I'm reminded in new and different situations about how I lock myself in old patterns. Met A the other day, walked by her work, and I realize that I get a bit stiff there too. Kind of like when I get addicted to the idea of other people liking me, I'm not acting like myself. I want the job, it's important, want to land it, but make things difficult. I want to meet and get to know A but make things difficult instead of making it easy.

When it comes to women, I'm thinking that I shouldn't think 'girlfriend' but just be myself and become friends first. Feels good to take it easy and not create any demands or expectations in me, or that anyone else expects anything from me except a good friend. Mm, and I've got to keep it simple there too, be honest, listen to myself, and have fun. Simply be me. To think that I should have to remind myself about this again and again. But I suppose it's a learning process and I'm glad that I know how to deal with it.

I now began to enter new situations, or old ones if you will, both regarding work and meeting women again. I had learnt a great deal but when I found myself in these new yet old situations, I easily slipped back into my old behavior. The situation was new for the new Thomas and that is why I slipped back. At the same time, I quickly gained perspective and

I now had the tools to find my way back. I guess this is what you mean when you talk about losing your head. You lose yourself.

It had been years since I dated, and it was a little painful to realize that I fell back to a nervous and insecure Thomas. I kept thinking that women expect the cool type, so I immediately lost my instincts and slipped back into an old behavior. At the same time, it was okay, I was learning all the time and quickly regained my perspective. This was another area in which I needed to find the simple Thomas and not put pressure on myself because "I must meet someone" but just move forward step by step. I wanted to get to know more people, more women, make more friends, and then time would show whether I found a girlfriend. In my experience, we guys often make it more difficult than it has to be; we think that women wants something else than what we really are. But when you think about it, you want the people you meet to be themselves, and thus you should be yourself too.

Thursday, November 2, 2017

The days are continuing to be interesting; I'm thinking about what to do about the assignment and my former employer. Got a proposal from my old employer that I can't agree to, it would mean that I couldn't run my own business. So, I said no thank you and told the client that I can't take the assignment.

I'm at the restaurant opposite from where I live and there are lots of people around. I felt like being around people tonight, grab some food and a beer or two. Good to just be among people, listening, seeing, feeling the positive bubbling energy.

I'm listening to a group of girls talking and it's interesting to hear just how they talk. One girl is telling something openly, the others listen patiently, and this is new somehow, but something I appreciate. I like to talk, to be listened to, and keep it simple. Without having to crack jokes, be alert, be interesting all the time, just share what I have to say in a simple way. Being here, listening to the girls and their openness and how they are friends. How can that become more of my reality, to relax more with my friends and share what I have to say?

I guess I should start by saying that I don't usually sit and eavesdrop on other people's conversations, but I was quickly drawn in by these three girls' conversation and how open and warm they were towards each other. One of them would start talking about how she felt and what was going on in her life, while the other two listened with interest and asked questions. They gave the speaker time and space to tell them how she was doing and feeling. It made me happy and a little warm inside to see how these three girls were there for each other, how they listened and shared, and I realized that they must have known each other for quite some time. And it made me think of myself, of my male friends and other men. What would the conversation be like? It wouldn't be the same at all. Why do men meet to talk about sports, interests, and other stuff? I cannot recall having experienced the same closeness as the girls were showing when I have conversed with my male friends.

I remember feeling like there wasn't any good occasions where you could talk about how you felt or what you were thinking about. When you were a teenager and started talking about something like that, you would get a whack on your shoulder and a "Don't be such a wuss" and so on. Today, I feel that many things should have been allowed to be brought up. Instead, there is a widespread unfamiliarity when it comes to talking about these deeper and personal things, and we don't know how to deal with it if the other person gets emotional. Am I just being extra sensitive? Am I the only man thinking like this? I don't think so, and regardless, I want more warmth and true dialogue with my male friends. I want to break the limiting male culture that says we must deal with everything ourselves and that we can't be vulnerable. We should be allowed to be there when a friend needs support. Thanks to these three girls, it has begun in me. When does it begin in you?

Monday, November 6, 2017

Today's reflection and last week's lesson: stand up for myself, do what feels right, and say no—that is, a yes to myself. By being a little "difficult" I've learned the importance of listening to myself, and I really got to practice staying calm in a real-life situation. It helped to think that it was a game, that it wasn't so serious. And to express my opinion, give feedback, listen to others, and then decide for me is absolutely okay. But it's tough, I'm not used to disagreement but usually give in because I don't want to be difficult. But as I said, a no is sometimes a yes to myself.

I just ran into my contacts from my former employer, and they seem positive after all. I thought they would be angry with me, that they would pursue me forever. Mm, I realize it's a game, we discuss a setup, but it isn't personal. It's good that I get to practice it. I feel calmer about the assignment this week, but it still takes energy. How does it get any better than this?

This was an incredibly challenging and exciting time, but I really stood up for myself. A lot of old feelings that had built up were about to be vented. A major part in the challenge about my former employer was the fact that I didn't stand up for myself back then. I gave in, and that was one of the reasons why I got burned out. I didn't express what I felt but just said yes to things. It was now very good to let that go and deal with these difficult things.

It was based on my childhood memories of receiving pain if I was being difficult. I took it very personally and thought that they would be angry with me. If I was difficult, they would pursue me forever and make my life miserable. This reminds me of my brother, of whom I was afraid when I was a child. I resolved situations and avoided fights because I knew how he would behave. My brother and I have talked about this, and he understands how I felt. It wasn't that we fought all the time; I became aware that it was a bad situation and acted before anything would happen. We were children but it has followed me, and to this day I am afraid of conflict. This situation obviously triggered much more in me than was warranted by the actual situation in the present. I think that it is sometimes good to think about whether you "overreact" to a situation. What does it trigger within you? Are there any memories or feelings that you have not dealt with that arise in different situations?

At the end of the day, I was very proud and glad that I stood up for what I wanted. I wanted to work with people who have the same mindset as I do. At the same time, being "difficult" towards my former employer gave me a better understanding of what they were worried about. We talked it through and straightened out how we looked at things. So, thanks to a little "difficulty", we resolved the conflict, dealt with things and got a better understanding of each other and could move on. I took the assignment with the client and my former employer accepted the setup. If I had accepted their first proposal, I would have been bitter and annoyed with them for a long time. I would have wasted energy and the conflict would have remained unresolved. If you avoid disagreement because you want to try and keep your calm, you instead start a war inside yourself. It is challenging to resolve disagreements, but they remain until they are resolved.

Sunday, November 12, 2017

This afternoon, I experienced a discharge I hadn't expected. I was watching a TV show and they talked about a certain song, and the lyrics say something about when it hurts so damned much and it means that you have a big heart, or an open heart. I broke down a little then and cried a lot. Guess I had a lot of tears dammed up after the week, and I felt almost like I got kicked by a horse. The calm I experienced afterwards told me to be the open and sensitive Thomas that I am. To let go of the whole thing with my old employer, and C, whom I also think affected me this week. It's been a lot this past week, and as I told my friend, I feel a bit confused, or like I'm seeing myself from the outside.

like I wanted to do something, didn't know what, just something; I was like a lost soul wandering around. At that point, it was easy to flip on the TV or check my phone in an attempt to unwind, but what I really needed then was to find my balance again. It takes a while and can be uncomfortable depending on what method you use, exercise or whatever, but after around 15–20 minutes, things will have calmed down. It is important to become aware of those times when you cannot calm down, when your mind starts to wander and you, almost unintentionally, try to unwind by getting more stimulus through your phone. That is when it is important to stop, recognize the pattern, take control, and do the things you need to do to actually unwind and recover. This is where you start to master your thoughts. It is important to find your tools or routines that help you unwind, especially when there is much else to do. And it is equally important to identify which of the things you already do that can be removed. I believe it has become more difficult to unwind, to do nothing, in our connected society. It is so easy to get "kicks" and give the brain more stimulus all the time. Can you identify with this? What do you do to unwind?

Tuesday, November 28, 2017

Almost time for bed… Feel that I've been a bit stressed and worried lately. My thoughts revolve around getting started on the assignment, what they expect, if they are satisfied, I want to finish so I can send the invoice. The project for my other client, create material. Events in the evenings. Do I have moths in my apartment? I saw some kind of bug. If that's the case, will I be thrown out of the apartment, is that how it works? Is my landlord unhappy with me, can I stay? Yes, a lot of thoughts are running away with me. But I took it easy this weekend. Talked to my old landlady from Eriksberg yesterday. Talking to her made me reconsider things and find my balance again. I have missed my me-time now that everything's up and running.

Sometimes I can laugh at myself a little when I enter different phases. It is as if I know that it has been too much. I get worried and my thoughts start spinning in all directions. I create lots of different scenarios in my head and everything keeps spinning. Even if it creates anxiety, it is a strength of mine to think about these things. Being resourceful, thinking of different alternatives, being creative, etc. However, when I am out of sync with myself, this ability brings with it a kind of anxiety, and I pick up on other people's negative energies. This is classic Thomas; as soon as someone is grumpy or angry around me, I think that it must be my fault. I take responsibility even though that person might just be having a bad day.

But I try to get better at this, and I learn all the time. I pick up on and become aware of different feelings, look at them and see if they belong to me. What causes these emotions? What should I react to? Sometimes I lose my calm and disappear into worries and thoughts. In the past, my head would be spinning when I lay in bed at night. Now, I use my techniques and tools. A lot of movement: a walk or some physical exercise. If it is late and I am going to bed, I do a little meditation or yoga. The important thing is to break the pattern and allow your thoughts and feelings to calm down and pass.

Saturday, December 2, 2017

Sitting on the couch at home, I'm soon off to a gig. Our second gig for a student orchestra here in town. Nice end to the week, managed to unwind. The meeting in Halmstad went well, I have kept working at my client's, and finished with a fun guest lecture at the Gothenburg University School of Business. Went to a party at Bar Italia, and then on Thursday to a dinner with "guy talk" which some guys in another band had set up. Thought about going to an After Work yesterday but when I got back from the lecture, I was too tired and enjoyed a quiet night at home instead.

Right now, I have a feeling of calm, tiredness, and satisfaction. So, it's time to rest and enjoy it. Have fun and feel good! Get away from the anxiety that came over me when I was feeling stressed. Do what I need at my part-time job and otherwise just take care of myself.

In the fall of 2017, the #metoo received much attention worldwide, and some of my acquaintances arranged a guy talk (#guytalk). It is a concept that was created by the gender equality foundation Make Equal[6] in the summer of 2016. The idea is to get men to talk more about equality, and to create a safe environment in which to talk about what it is like to be a man in different contexts. It is a very important theme and a good environment in which we men can test the ground and talk about different subjects. The talk uses different themes, and you can find downloadable manuals on their website which guide the conversation and offer advice. There were fourteen of us and we got together several times in the fall, always around a good dinner. We had very good discussions and I noticed how valuable it was to both talk about important matters and have the open environment in which everybody was brave enough to talk.

In my experience, the discussion sometimes gets stuck around the point that not "all men" behave badly, but I think it is wrong to focus on who is right or wrong. To me, it is all about us men having a responsibility to stand up for a broader definition of masculinity and manliness. If we men allow shitty attitudes and sexist talk to be used and don't speak up—then we are tacitly approving of it. Simple as that. And that is the point: we need to speak up and say that it is not okay. In that regard, these guy talks gave us strength, because we realized that there are a lot of us who don't like that kind of talk, and we all recognized the challenge in finding the courage to speak up. The so-called *hierarchy of sexism* is sometimes used to illustrate how this kind of language escalates and leads to inequality, harassment, and violence/abuse. So, if we men take

---

6   Make Equal is a Swedish foundation that works for gender equality and offers lectures and workshops, as well as a "gender equality certificate" for companies and organizations. Make Equal has won a number of awards. More information about #guytalk can be found at www.killmiddag.se.

our mutual responsibility and make sure to show our disapproval when we encounter those attitudes, we can tear down that hierarchy and in its stead build a better society. And it isn't only about sexism and harassment—macho attitudes between men and derogatory talk must also be stopped early. In all likelihood, most of the people in any given group feel that it isn't okay, but nobody is willing to speak up because they believe they are alone—but I think we are in the majority. If you feel that you don't stand for such attitudes, say so! Break the pattern! The more people who speak up, the sooner we will get there.

Another benefit of the concept of guy talk is that we can help each other prepare for the conversations we will have later with our friends. During these dinners, a safe space was created and many of the participants felt stronger as they later were able to talk about things with their other male friends. I hope it will turn into a wave, that we begin to talk more about deep areas and different perspectives. On the #guytalk website, it is stated that one in five men lacks a close friend, and that 70 % of suicides are men. There is much that men need to work on, and starting to talk more can be a first step. This is something that the American Psychological Association put forth in their latest guidelines for how psychologists should deal with boys and men (*Guidelines for Psychological Practice with Boys and Men*, August 2018). In this report, which took 13 years to compile and is based on 40 years of research, it is shown that "traditional masculinity—marked by stoicism, competitiveness, dominance and aggression—is, on the whole, harmful" and that "socializing boys to suppress their emotions causes damage that echoes both inwardly and outwardly." Men who socialize and behave in this traditional masculine way are less likely to adopt healthy behaviors.

Even if #guytalk is a very good initiative, I think we have to start earlier if we are to see a real change in broader society, because this "macho culture"—if you will—is already established in childhood. In the book *Raise an Emotionally Healthy Boy* by Ted Zeff, the author brings up a study showing the differences in how boys and girls express emotions. In this study, it was observed that as infants, boys and girls cry equally when they are frustrated—but at age five, most boys have suppressed almost all emotions except anger. Yet even if the boys are socialized to control their emotions, the study shows that they actually react to the emotions with increased heart rate or sweaty palms just like the girls. Thus, we guys have the same emotions but we "aren't allowed" to show that we are afraid or sad—what we are "allowed" to show is anger. You don't have to be a rocket scientist or a psychologist to see that this will have consequences when the boys become teens and adults, both for themselves individually and for society. What is it that holds us back, and can we begin to change now? I believe this is already changing when I look at children today, but I still think this is something we really need to be aware of and bring up for discussion. If we are to truly master our emotions—all of them—we need to start talking about what happens on the inside, start putting our emotions into words. What can you do to help our children and your male friends to be brave enough to talk when they need to?

Sunday, December 10, 2017

Sunday night and it's been a nice weekend. Up and down this week, felt good but a little anxious about losing stuff, my client, the apartment, etc. Just because it feels good, something will probably go wrong… But what if it isn't so, what if things can just be good and I'm worth it ☺

My friend Lotta says that she can tell a difference in that I am much more calm and harmonious now. And I do feel calm and I'm doing well. But I can sometimes lose it when I'm with a client. When I'm in a dependent position, I sometimes get anxious, as if someone will pull the rug out from under me and rob me of the apartment, my job, etc. Like they would say, "We don't want you anymore; now that you've been here and we see who you are, we'll throw you out because you're not good enough." It's not true, but it is the basis of my anxiety. What do I need to make it feel good? Whatever feels easy is right, I must allow myself to relax. Things can always happen and change, but I must believe that people like me in the same way as I like them. Be calm, listen… Mm, be calm and listen even more, I think, and that's what I like to do. Ask more questions, not be pushy and driven. Have faith in my experience in what I do. The things that are easy for me might not be easy for others. I need to realize that I have learned a lot and show respect when other people can't easily see what can I see—in the same way as I can't see and understand what others do.

Keep it simple, have fun, and be helpful. Simply feel good! Grateful for everything around me! How does it possibly get any better than this?

I now truly felt that things began to settle, and that my friends noticed the difference in me. It was good to feel the calm. At the same time, I experienced anxiety again about things disappearing when I am doing too well, as if I don't deserve to be well. I felt that things should be hard and that if I felt good, something should disappear—especially if I expressed happiness over my success or celebrated it. These were familiar thoughts and I now used my questions to sort things out. What was behind the fear? Step by step, I created order among my thoughts and worries. I chose to acknowledge whatever came up, but I did not cling to the idea or feeling. I sorted it out and kept my head clear.

Sunday, December 17, 2017

Feeling philosophical and calm today. It's been a nice weekend, Mom and Jan came visiting. They arrived on Friday and in the evening, the boys came over too, and we had tacos and a good night. On Saturday, I went for a walk on Amund Island, and I could vent some tension from last week. I needed some me-time and nature. Later that day, we celebrated my mom's 65th birthday and combined it with a Christmas smorgasbord.

On Wednesday, I'm finally going to Australia, and I will relax, have fun, and go on adventures. I like ☺

Wednesday, December 20, 2017

I'm now on the plane to Abu Dhabi, where I will make a stopover before the flight to Australia. Feels incredible to be on the way. Yesterday, when everything was to be prepared and the apartment cleaned before my land-lord arrived, I was calm. Even went to yoga at 7:30. Nice to get that done on the night before departure.

Good finish to my assignment, made my delivery and finished with a lunch with my client, and it felt like a good closure. Monday was also good, with meetings and a concert with the boys in the evening. Great night!

But now, as I said, I'm very relaxed and calm. It feels great to be on the way. I haven't planned that much what I will do and that feels good. First, I'll spend three days at Emily's in Perth and then around ten days at Andy's in Bunbury. Then I'll see, depends on whether I get any good leads, otherwise I reckon I'll go to Sydney. It really doesn't matter, just want to be there, take it easy, and see what happens.

Thought about a thing my yoga instructor said yesterday, to straighten my back, both at yoga and in life. I feel that there's truth in that, to take my place. Talk calmly and from the stomach, believe in what I do and stand up for it. Straighten my back and take my place. The project and the assignment reminded me that I give in, become nervous, and make a bad impression. I'm not being honest with myself.

This is an interesting perspective, if I look back over the years. I think about my time working at Volvo. The anxiety there and then the next com-pany. Although, Volvo had many aspects, energy and creativity, the large project was amazing, but then at the end things got tough. It was fun at my last employer for about three years but then it changed. My first serious relationship, I'm able to take away the feeling of being in a long relationship. Marriage and stepchildren with C, I bring a lot with me from that and feel stronger as a person, like I'm capable of doing more.

It feels like I've always underestimated myself, thinking that I'm not good enough, then adapting—and it's true. But why do I think of that now... Feels like my new self, after burnout and the turbulent years, is returning to the same pattern when I come back to work and need to deliver. My experiences from the last two years disappear and I become insecure again.

It is interesting that I fall back into my old patterns workwise, when I'm calm and liking it in other contexts. And it's in that calm space I should be. Good that the assignment is finished, otherwise it would've drained all my energy. Need to focus on what I like. I also think about the rhetoric, to be calm in my body language and voice. I often fall into a stressed mode and my speech is physically shallow. Don't always have to talk, take the initiative. Show with body language, keep my voice calm, show interest, listen to others, open up and just be. I'll practice that in Australia.

We need to straighten our backs in life, be proud of who we are and what we do. We need to throw off the limiting Law of Jante (if you don't know what this is, google it and you will gain an insight into the mindset of most Scandinavians). It has nothing to do with us thinking that we are better than anyone else; it is about doing the things that make us feel good and that we have the aptitude for. If we feel that we do that which we believe in, we should do it with all the energy we have. We should stand up for and be confident in what we believe in. We should also take responsibility for our emotions and our own personal development, as well as for our behavior and actions. If there is a discussion about any of it, listen, absorb the information you receive, and see if you can learn anything. Just because someone else thinks something else, it doesn't mean that you are wrong. You don't have to change to fit their ideas if you believe in yourself. And if you receive useful information that helps you get further, take it to heart.

It sometimes feels like we have to think the same, and do the same to fit in. But what if we could focus on doing our own things? We don't need to come to a consensus about everything. We can disagree; we can discuss the matter at hand. It is perfectly okay to have interesting and intense discussions, and we can disagree. We can learn from each other, gain new perspectives. We can even agree to disagree. And then we part as friends. I sometimes feel that we are afraid of that kind of discussion. Perhaps you don't agree? Perhaps it has to do with our Swedish fear of disagreement and our inclination towards always striving for consensus?

Tuesday, December 26, 2017

Boxing Day, and I'm at a beachfront café in Bunbury. It's been a quiet day, good to have some time to get settled. When I arrived in Bunbury on Sunday, which was Christmas Eve, Andy picked me up at the train station. Then we went to a restaurant by the water, grabbed a beer, and met one of his friends. Later, after we had left my luggage at his place, we went for a swim in the sea, then I ran a bit and, in the evening, we had a barbecue by the sea and watched the sunset.

On Christmas Day, we went for a hike and a swim in the sea before we went to his family and celebrated with his sister and her children and grandchildren. A fun day, and before we went to his sister's, we visited his father's farm. Today, the plan was to go on a 2.5-hour trip, but we changed the plans as I felt I needed a quiet day. I get overwhelmed by all the input, and it takes a lot of energy just to get my English going. Everybody is really nice but sometimes it just gets too much. I'm exhausted and my brain feels full ☺ So, this morning Andy went to a café and I went for a walk and did some yoga by the sea. It was great!!!

It's tricky sometimes when you're a guest, people offer you things and they mean well, but it's too much to take in. It was good that I mentioned yesterday that I was tired, because Andy understood.

Looking forward to a joyful new year with a lot of fun. How does it possibly get any better than this!? ☺

Australia = dream trip and I'm here!!!

Even if this was the trip of my dreams, I needed time for reflection and pause. Things were wonderful but it could still get too much, and I couldn't take anymore in. I guess we are different when we are on vacation. Some people want to do as much as possible—including me—but in order to absorb everything, I need some downtime too.

I listened to myself here too and told my host I needed some me-time. And of course, it wasn't a problem for him. He did other things. I realized that it wouldn't have been nice of me if I had gone along without enjoying it. What if he had asked me if I liked it and I had said that I really just wanted to have taken it easy. It wouldn't have been nice if he had taken the time to arrange everything, spent his time on showing me around while all I wanted was to take a break. I think this is another area in which we need to be more honest and speak up. It is kinder to express what you really want instead of thinking that you are being kind by going along. At the very least, there will be a discussion and an openness about what you want.

Sunday, December 31, 2017

Happy new year!

Last day of 2017. Began the day with a walk on the beach and some yoga, great start! Yesterday, I was at a wine tasting the whole day. It was a lot of fun going out, meeting some new people, a fun guided tour through three vineyards, a chocolate tasting, cheese tasting, and a brewery. Yesterday also began with a walk and yoga.

How am I feeling? Pretty okay, a little tired and exhausted. Thinking that I should do more stuff and at the same time I just want to take it easy. So, the plan now is to just relax for a couple of days. Read, hang out at the beach, go cycling. Take one day at a time, enjoy the nice weather. Move my body, do yoga, run, cycle, and eat healthy.

I feel fine now and am very proud of the journey I've made. Proud of the honesty towards myself. All the lessons, steps I've taken to learn. My trips to Rome, El Camino, Australia, and the yoga retreats. Starting my own business. Moving twice. That both apartments have been great and given me new acquaintances and friends.

I am proud over how I've opened up and gotten close to a lot of people. Friends, family, old colleagues, and new acquaintances. How great is that? I lost it a bit in Nov–Dec when it got a bit tough again and my energy level went down. Glad that that assignment was finished as it opens up for new ones. I'm glad that I'm now traveling and have some time off to just take care of myself. This is the trip of my dreams, I've made it happen, and I don't need a bunch of have tos. I'm here to enjoy myself and recover!! Don't have to optimize my time here to see as much as possible. I'll just do whatever feels good and enjoy being here.

I choose to end my story here, on the other side of the planet, after three transforming years. The transformation began when I noticed and started to break the patterns I had, which created anxiety and a negative self-image. I then built up the feeling that I am okay just the way I am, and I thought about why I felt bad. I listened to the feelings that told me my body had to feel good, that something had to happen. Thanks to the change in habits, with more physical exercise and a healthier diet, I gave my body the chance to recover. It gave me energy and time for reflection. It felt unfamiliar to break habits, but I had made up my mind; this was what I wanted, and I knew it was good for me. And when I began to notice the positive changes, it gave me even more energy to continue in the same direction. Opening up, being brave enough to be vulnerable, and beginning to talk about my thoughts with my close friends made it easier to break my thought patterns. Thanks to that initial openness and honesty, I found my way into more positive and open environments. In these new environments, with new friends, I was brave enough to open my heart. I listened to other people's stories, and suddenly I wasn't alone with my thoughts. That allowed me to change my thought patterns and let go of things from my emotional backpack. Childhood memories which had limited me as an adult could now be gotten rid of. I allowed myself to face my innermost fears, the stuff that lay hidden and buried in my subconscious. I began to accept my thoughts and ruminations and allowed myself to be who I am.

2017 was one of the toughest and simultaneously the easiest year I have ever experienced. The grief over breaking up and leaving a relationship and a family, and simultaneously the joy in being myself to the fullest and doing things I had thought about for a long time. Today, I feel stronger and more complete as a person. I know that life goes up and down, stuff happens, both positive and negative. I know how to handle it now, how I should look at life, and how I choose to handle whatever happens. I choose to live my life to the fullest as I am.

Today, I also have the courage to talk about what is on my mind, feelings and things that I previously have considered "wrong" to bring up. My thoughts and feelings are energies and I view them differently. I keep it simple and think that whatever happens is just *there*, there is no right or wrong. I don't judge myself but instead see it as information, and then make different choices. In the same way, I don't judge anyone else and think that it is their fault that I feel a certain way. Instead, I think, "All right, this is how it feels right now, there is no right or wrong about it, what can we do to make it better?"

I am kinder towards myself and allow myself to do more of the things I like and that comes easy for me. I am also kind towards myself by saying no to things and people that don't give me energy. I am open, and if other people don't want to be open back, well, then it is their choice as grown-ups. I am here but it is up to everyone else how they want to act and feel. If I act differently towards others, it is okay, as long as I am being honest towards myself.

I know my body and my head when it comes to what I need to feel well. I absorb a lot of information and like to ponder different things. Sometimes it gets too much and then I need my calm. When I had a lot to do in the past, I skipped exercise because I thought there wasn't time. Now, it is almost the other way around; if I have lots to do and things are tough, I need to exercise and relax more to make it through. I have found the forms of exercise that suit me: a mix of running, yoga, and going to the gym. Walking and being present in nature are also important parts of my everyday life. When I have a lot going on, I avoid stimulus from TV and large crowds. It isn't relaxing for me to watch TV. What I need is less stimulus.

By being more honest towards myself, I also allow other people to be exactly who they are. We all have our own journey and our own baggage. I listen with curiosity and a relaxed attitude. I allow other people to have their feelings; I don't absorb them, but I can help others to let go of them if they want to. I allow other people to have their opinions and experiences. I listen with awareness to learn more about myself. If someone is judging me or others, and I see that it is really their own unprocessed feelings, I don't take that onboard. That kind of judgement has more to do with them than with me. If I were to listen to everybody's opinions and thoughts, it would get very difficult. Everybody has the right to their own opinion, and I have the right to mine.

In close relationships, it is all about showing respect and actively or reflectively listening. In the past, I wouldn't dare bring up small matters because I thought I was being difficult. I thought that if I were to talk about this or that, then the relationship would end, or if I talked to a friend, I would lose her or him. But what I have realized is that by sharing more, I get closer to other people. I have learned that by being more of me, more honest and open, I allow others to be more relaxed and more themselves. In my experience, many people harbor the same thoughts and anxieties, but we don't have the courage to talk about them. What if we were brave enough to talk more and discover that we are more alike than we think, and can help each other more? What kind of world could we create then?

I am very grateful for the insights I have gained. I realize how I have put limitations upon my own life. Because I have shut off my emotions and got stuck in doing things I thought were expected of me, I have lost relationships. I thought that by avoiding talking about how I felt, I could keep the relationship. But the conflict was there anyway, and it remained unresolved for too long. Now, I have let go of the past and forgiven myself for the limitations I have put upon myself. I now bring things up in a simpler way. I use the faith in my feelings; I bring up thoughts and feelings without being judgmental. I listen to feedback from others without taking a defensive position or running away. It makes it easier to talk about all kinds of matters. I need to keep practicing talking, and I guess we are all in different stages. I now experience a greater closeness and openness with my friends and family. I am incredibly happy and grateful for the difference and for how much more each encounter provides today.

I am no longer afraid to feel too much; instead, my sensitivity and vulnerability are allowed to exist, and I am stronger for it. It makes me feel more alive, I see more nuance, and am brave enough to enjoy life to the fullest.

How does it get any better than this? ☺

CHAPTER 15

Conclusion

Thank you for wanting to read my book and sharing my journey, these thoughts and reflections. I hope that this gives you new ideas, thoughts, energy, and courage to take on the changes you want in life. If you want to start something, if you want to break free, do so, it is your life and your choice. I have chosen to be very open with my own vulnerability. My experience of leadership courses, self-help books, and novels tells me that it might seem easy to absorb and intellectually understand how and what you should do to feel well. The challenge is to move on from there, to actually have the courage to try, to allow yourself to fall and pick yourself up again. To meet your inner world, your fears, your thoughts, your emotions, what is actually happening on the inside that stops you. And perhaps it is the inner journey that is the most important. And it is indeed the journey that I wanted to share, and how I truly felt when I took the first faltering steps towards reclaiming my life.

One of the most important things I have learned over the last couple of years is that I am not alone in my thoughts and ruminations. By listening to other people's stories and seeing their courage when they enter the arena and reveal their vulnerability, I have found the courage to embark on new adventures myself. I have understood the importance of an emotionally safe environment and realized that everybody is strong enough to move on in their own way. It is my hope that you can see my journey, my challenge, my breaking patterns as an inspiration. You have your history, your emotional backpack, your challenges, just as I have mine. As I said at the start of the book, I am sharing my own experiences in the hope that you will find them helpful on your journey. I also hope that you now feel inspired to take new steps in your life, to start talking about the things that matter, to listen to your feelings, and to find the people with whom you can share your experiences. Take care of the people around you, maintain an emotionally safe space, and be brave enough to be yourself.

If you, the reader, are a man, I hope that you see that we men can invite so much more into our lives. By opening up and having the courage to talk about feelings and thoughts, no matter how difficult they are, you will rather quickly realize that you are not as alone as you think. Take heart and dare talk—together, we can help each other. I also hope that you see how our legacy of certain masculine norms is limiting. These norms turn us into lonely creatures, and we forget somehow that we are really people with emotions, doubts, and thoughts. The hard armor we sometimes put on is more restrictive than strengthening. It is my firm belief that we can make a real difference in society if we lift our eyes and think about how we want our children to grow up and live. Men who care do not create an uncaring society. Vulnerable men are strong men.

With this book, I have challenged myself and at times it has been tough to be so open. At the same time, it has been incredibly liberating to let go and be brave enough to share things that I have kept inside for a very long time. For most of my life, I have had a wall to protect me and I never shared how I truly felt. I have been asked what it is like to share my diary, to share my inner thoughts and lay myself bare. My answer is that I am not my feelings. What you read here are feelings that have passed through me, but they are not me. By letting go of my old limitations, I make room for new experiences to pass through me, and I am open to whatever life brings me.

Finally, I realize that I have always been okay. I have family and friends who like me, and they always have. There has been an anxiety, an insecurity, an inadequacy in close relationships, but that has all been on me. In my subconscious, I have carried old truths that were created long ago. If you carry similar anxieties, thoughts, and fears, think about what changes you want to make. You can learn more about yourself, break your patterns, understand your reactions, your feelings and their history. By doing that, you can master your emotions and create an inner peace and balance. Life is a journey, and always changing. What steps do you want to take to reclaim your life and live it to the fullest?

CHAPTER 16

Acknowledgements

There are so many people to thank for the creation of this book. You know who you are. I would like to lift a few people who have supported me a little extra and made sure that I got started. Ina Elverljung and Malin Sandell at Högkänslighet Sverige. Thank you for being here, you have supported me for so long and given me energy and inspiration to create. My coach and kick in the rear Marianne Fröberg. Thank you for your challenging coaching and for providing me with a writer's lodge for my creative writing. Lovisa Mellgren for your inspiration and your support as an independent consultant, and for teaching me to find my own place and time. Carl Ahlstrand for your support and knowledge about how a book is created, with structure, concept, and language, and for translating the book into English. Lina Bodestad for your support and psychological perspective on my story and HSP. Jonas Freeman for your support and focus during the finishing touches. My brother and his family, for being there. Carl and Nanna for your standing invitation to see the kids, many cups of coffee, and your patient listening to the progress of my book. My friends at the HSP life coaching education for brainstorming, support, and providing me with a space in which I could be vulnerable when things were tough.

My stepchildren—I am your stepdad now and forever; thanks for everything you always bring!

Finally, Mom and Dad, thank you for being here. Your support during my writing, your input and reflections, and for how we, thanks to this process, have come even closer together.

CHAPTER 17

Self-Reflection Workbook

Here at the end of the book, I have chosen to collect a few areas of reflection for you to work through, either on your own or in a group—for example, your friends or family. Each area for reflection has a short introduction, and then there are a number of questions for solo reflection and direct questions for group discussions. View it as a start, an introduction, and use whatever suits you at the time. Always, if you are unsure and it feels too much, please seek professional help. To me, these are subjects and questions that have helped me understand myself better, and subjects that I have felt are very good to discuss with other people. When I have discussed these questions with others and shared my own story, it has created an openness between us. Because I have exposed myself—shown myself as vulnerable—we have grown closer.

So, take these questions with you. If you read them by yourself, I recommend that you write down your answers, because putting your thoughts into words make them more real. Otherwise, talk to your partner, your friends, colleagues, or family. If you ever feel like talking to a professional psychologist or therapist, do that. Find your way to begin talking, and learn to understand yourself better, your patterns and the steps you need to take to grow more as yourself.

When you talk as a group, it is important that you first put up some ground rules and create a safe space based on trust. What do you expect from each other? Do you want to keep whatever you talk about in the group? Then discuss it first. Try to avoid solving someone else's problem; ask questions instead and trust that the person talking is capable of solving their own problems. You can be like a torch, using your curious questions to light up and help your friends see what they could not see before. Be humble, for we are not all used to talking about sensitive things. Take care of each other. Remember that the person who opens up can quickly retreat into their shell again like a tortoise and remain there. As I said, take care of each other, and allow yourselves to be the wonderfully sensitive creatures you are.

This can be a challenging exercise if you are not used to dealing with emotions. I was definitely unaccustomed to it, and it was difficult for me to begin facing those emotions. Be prepared that it might be difficult but let it be uncomfortable. Remember that emotions are energies, they usually pass through your body and disappear in a couple of minutes. My advice if you begin to feel uncomfortable—close your eyes. Breathe all the way down into your stomach. Feel *where* in your body the uncomfortable feeling is. Drop your chin and relax your facial muscles. Breathe calmly. Think that the uncomfortable feeling is like smoke that rises through your body from that spot. The smoke should rise, through your chest and throat and be allowed to pass up into your head. Cry, scream, laugh, do whatever you have to do. And for the people who sit beside the person experiencing this discomfort, allow that person to be sad, believe in the process and just be there and give your friend the space to be vulnerable for a moment.

DISCERNING PATTERNS

I got stuck in a lot of things and musts that I thought I needed to feel good. I had a well-paid job, a successful career. I had a house, a wife, and I helped a lot of other people. When I talked to others, I told them all was well, I kept the façade up and didn't want them to know how I really felt. We are all different in this regard; some have goals they want to accomplish; others know exactly how it should feel.

I began to see different patterns in me which made me feel bad. I was stuck, but I was beginning to receive signals and feel that I wanted to have something else from life. I began to see that I played different roles to fit in. There was a feeling of dejection and inadequacy. When I looked closer at my health, I saw that I wasn't eating healthily. I stressed at home and at work. Simply put, I wasn't feeling well. My friend told me that, "You should be Thomas" and I was reminded about how I used to feel. It can be different—I had been well before and that meant I could be well again. I began to notice and change my habitual patterns.

Patterns in your wellbeing

- Do you feel that you can be yourself when you are with your closest family? At work/school? Among friends? Is it different in different contexts?
- What do you think about being adequate, being good enough? What does that mean to you?
- How do you usually feel when you are at home?
- How do you usually feel when you are at work/school?
- How do you perceive your wellbeing now compared to previously?
- Has your life changed in any way that affects your wellbeing today? How?
- How do you perceive the balance between time to yourself and time you spend with other people?

Norms, musts, and expectations

- What different roles do you play in your life today and how do you like those roles?
- What norms about being successful can you see today? What "shoulds" and "musts" have been imposed upon you?
- Which "shoulds" and "musts" do you like today, and which would you like to change?
- What usually happens to you when you have too much to do? How do you handle it?
- How would you like it to be?
- If you could choose, what would you like to have more of in your life three years from now?

EXPLORE YOUR PATTERNS AND YOUR EMOTIONAL RESPONSES

I began to break my patterns because I realized something had to be done if I was going to feel better. Gradually, I began to talk about how I felt, and I found helpful advice on how to change. Thanks to this help and the understanding of the HSP trait, I began to allow myself to be me. Through conversations with Ina and group sessions at the HSP retreats, I gained even more understanding of myself, and I understood my reactions and actions.

Now, I want you to be kind to yourself. If you begin to judge yourself, saying that you should have realized things sooner—pause. You are where you are at this moment; allow yourself to be here. You are okay just the way you are. View everything that has happened up until this point as information, a background as to why you are here now. Get to know yourself, review your own history, begin to explore with curiosity in order to understand yourself on a deeper level.

Dealing with stress and accepting help from others

For me, it took a long time before I admitted to myself that I had been burned out, that I had been ill. I also realize that I caught it in time, before I suffered even worse symptoms—which unfortunately many people do. It still went far, because, "I'm not a guy who gets ill." I am strong and the one who helps others. With the perspective I have now, I can see that there were even earlier signals that I failed to recognize. For example, I thought things like, "Why do I get tired, everyone else can do it, I guess there's something wrong with me" and, "I should be able to keep up with every-thing." I also thought that, "I'll just keep going until Christmas, until the vacation, then I will rest." But that rest didn't always come as I had hoped.

- Can you identify with the feeling that small, everyday things like taking out the trash or doing the dishes can feel like insur-mountable obstacles? If so, how do you handle it?
- How do you sleep? Do you have trouble falling asleep, do you wake up early, are things spinning around inside your head?
- What signals do your body send you, telling you to pause? Do you listen to your body and its signals?
- What strategy do you use to prioritize among the things you have to do? When is it difficult to prioritize, and when is it easy?
- What do you think about accepting help and needing other people? How do you usually handle it when you need help with something?

If you can identify with my description or if you feel stressed, read up on burnout/exhaustion syndrome. Pause. Talk to your family, friends, or coworkers.

Recovery

- What do you do when you feel tired and weary? How do you recharge your batteries, how do you recover?
- What tools do you use to feel good and unwind?
- What kind of physical exercise do you like best and what works for you?
- What kind of mental recovery/exercise works best for you? What would you like to do more of?
- What more would you need to recover mentally and physically?
- What would the first step towards more physical and mental recovery be for you?

Choose for you/time to yourself

I have always sacrificed myself for others. If anyone has asked me for help, I have tried to help them—even if I had planned or needed to do something else. At the same time, I didn't ask for help myself or think about what I needed to feel well. Sacrificing yourself and always doing things for other people is also a factor that contributes to burnout.

- How important is it for you to be helpful, even if you have to ignore your own needs?
- How often do you choose to help others when you have other plans? Try to describe the last time you chose to prioritize someone else above yourself.
- What are you afraid will happen if you were to say no when someone asks for your help and you can't or won't help? Describe that feeling. Can you see where that feeling comes from?
- What do you think of people who say no when they can't or won't?
- If you had more time to yourself, what would you do and how would that feel?
- How do you think your partner/family/friends would view you if you chose to be by yourself? What do you think they would say?

If you are going to be able to help people in the long run, you also need to take care of yourself. If an airplane loses cabin pressure, you are supposed to help yourself with the oxygen mask first before you help anyone else. What if the same is true in life? I don't believe that you can help others if you are losing oxygen. How do you choose for you?

Mastering emotions and cleaning out the emotional backpack

I experienced better confidence and better self-knowledge when I began to understand my emotions and thoughts. I began to understand why the feelings came, why I got angry and irritable. I could see what I didn't do, what I wasn't brave enough to talk about, and eventually it became too much, and I got angry.

Understanding myself and learning to manage my thoughts and emotions was a major key. To me, it is like keeping my head tidy. It means sorting my thoughts and emotions, cleaning out whatever is there, and airing it out so that I can let things go. I chose yoga, meditation, physical exercise, and nature as my tools.

The emotional management also helped me let go of and understand old feelings that I had carried with me for a long time. I call this "baggage" my emotional backpack—and I believe we all have one, since we all carry a lot with us, perhaps especially from childhood, that we haven't dealt with enough or that we don't see. (The emotional backpack is also a process; the more you take out, the more you find that you didn't know was there—emotions, behaviors, and memories that you had forgotten.) When I began to sort through the backpack, one thing I saw was that I had learned certain behaviors as a teenager, for example how I acted in a group or how to avoid confrontations. I had learned that it hurts when someone leaves me, and that is why, later in life, I chose not to open myself to love. If my emotional backpack had been opened and sorted earlier, I expect my life would have looked very different.

I told you earlier about how I cleaned out my storage, which was filled to the brim with stuff, and how step by step I got rid of things, making me feel lighter. It was the same with my emotions when I sorted through them. These emotions had helped me in the past—25, 15, or 5 years ago—but they were limiting me today. In middle school, among pubescent teenagers and ugly curse words, my emotions and behavior were a defense. But that is not the case today; it is not the same environment and I don't need the same defenses when I am among grown-ups.

- How do emotions usually express themselves in you and how do you manage them?
- What emotions are there in your backpack that you want to get rid of? What do you carry that might have worked before but is limiting you today?
- Is there anything that limits you today and keep you from living the life you want to live? If so, how does it express itself?
- How do you feel right now?
- What do you think is behind that feeling?
- What would happen if you let that feeling out?
- How would it feel if you allowed that feeling to pass?
- When you have vented feelings, now or earlier, how does it feel afterwards?

You have now gone deeper into yourself. Hopefully, it has awakened new thoughts. You can come back to these questions whenever you feel lost. Use the questions in your everyday life. What happened now? What is behind that emotion? I am stressed, why is that? That will help you to understand your reactions and master your emotions, see why and how you react, and you can be more prepared for similar experiences in the future.

VULNERABILITY

To be more of you, you need to be vulnerable. Allow yourself to be who you are. Then you also show others that they can be themselves around you. They don't need a wall, because they know that you like them just the way they are. How can it get any better than that? ☺

Lowering the wall

I felt very alone with my thoughts, but the more I talked about it with others, the more I learned that many people have similar thoughts. What if you are not alone with your thoughts? My family, friends, and acquaintances have been through grief, divorce, doubts, broken hearts, and so on. In my experience the more I open up and show my vulnerability to my friends, the more I create an emotionally safe environment in which others can be open with how they feel. We don't judge each other; we allow each other to be ourselves.

- Do you sometimes feel different, like there are things that only you think about? If so, give a couple of examples.
- Has a person close to you shown their emotions and been vulnerable with you? How did you handle that?
- Did that affect how you view that person? If so, how?
- What would you need from the people closest to you to be brave enough to talk more about how you feel?
- How would it feel to be able to talk about it and be vulnerable?
- How do you think other people would view you if you were vulnerable and showed your feelings?
- Is there someone with whom you can talk about anything and everything? If not, with whom would you like to talk?
- Do you think that there is a gender difference regarding exposing your thoughts and being vulnerable? How would you like it to be?

Listening and being there for others

In my experience, we sometimes make things more difficult than they have to be when we talk to each other. We think that we are there to solve someone else's problem or that we don't want to bother them with questions. But what if you contribute simply by being there, listening to your friend. Your presence in itself is a contribution, creating a safe space. You see your friend, you listen, and allow your friend to be vulnerable and open. You can ask questions, be a guiding light, and help your friend see things from a new perspective. Take your friend's feelings seriously, give them space to be fragile.

- What would you want to talk more about that you don't talk about today?
- What stops you from being vulnerable?
- How would you want others to react when you tell them about something that is difficult for you?
- What kind of questions do you prefer to get when you talk about the difficult stuff?
- How would it feel if someone gets emotional? What would be uncomfortable and what would feel good? What would happen if you were simply there and allowed your friend to be sad?
- How do you handle it when/if your partner is vulnerable and open to you?
- When someone tells you they feel bad, how do you want to help that person?

Talking about feelings

When I grew up, I felt that it wasn't okay for men to show their feelings or to be vulnerable. And I see the same thing today, at least in part. There is a kind of inexperience when it comes to dealing with emotions, both when talking about one's own feelings and when listening to someone else being emotional. We are simply not used to it, and we men can become much better at it.

It would have been better if I could have talked earlier, when I was young, and then have gained an understanding of my emotions. It would also have been good if my family and other grown-ups would have had the understanding to identify with my situation. I think it is easy for an adult to give quick answers, but when it comes to emotions, it is all about learning to understand yourself at your own pace. Quick answers can make you retreat because you feel that they don't understand you.

- How did people around you talk about and view emotions when you grew up? What has been okay and what has not been okay?
- What do you think it would be like in your family/circle of friends if you were more emotionally safe, willing to express your feelings and letting others express theirs? And if everybody was more willing to let emotions be expressed—what would society look like?
- What would you need in order to be more vulnerable and talk more about feelings?
- If you are a parent, how do you talk to your child/children about facing and managing emotions?

Norms around men and masculinity

In my experience, there are norms and unstated expectations about us men that aren't really working anymore. I believe these norms are detrimental to our health because they don't allow us to be vulnerable and talk about difficult things. We must break the macho norm, for our children, for women, and for ourselves, so that we can feel better. Men who feel well treat others well.

- What do you think a man should be like for others to like him?
- What kind of language was used at your school?
- What kind of language is used in the different contexts you are in today, e.g. at work, among friends, playing sports, or at the gym?

- Can you see any gender differences regarding which emotions are more or less okay to express and show others?
- What kind of masculine norms do you see today? What is positive and negative about them?
- What would we gain from tearing down the macho norm?

Fear

What if you could view fear as information? Something happens that you are not used to, and you enter an active state. I use questions in such situations, for example: What is behind this? What am I afraid of and what do I want to do? Imagine that the fear can give you the energy you need to break free from something old and move towards something new.

- How do you view fear?
- In what ways do fear affect you today?
- Do you sometimes feel limited by fear? In what context?
- Have you ever used your fear to move on to something new? If so, how did you do it and what did you learn from it?

Taking your own life:
breaking the taboo and talking before it is too late

Right at the start of this book, I am open with the fact that there have been moments when I have thought about ending my own life. Unfortunately, talking about suicide is still a very charged subject, even taboo. I didn't have the courage to talk about my thoughts and feelings—not even with my closest family. Because how would they react and view me then? Suicide is an absolute last way out, and there are so many layers of thoughts and emotions on top of the suicidal thoughts. I believe that if we got better at being open about our most difficult thoughts and feelings, we would be able to help each other find other ways out, even from our darkest places.

A safe environment in which to talk is needed when addressing this subject, so the first step is to create such an environment. What people would you like to address this subject with? See if you can invite these people to a discussion, either all at once or one at a time.

Once you have established the framework for the discussion, you can start with one of the following questions:

- Have you ever felt that it would be better for the people around you if you didn't exist? What did your life look like when you had those thoughts?
- Was there someone you could talk to about those feelings? How did you deal with those feelings?
- Can you distinguish a pattern that makes you feel bad and have those thoughts?
- What do you need to break that pattern and feel better?
- How do you usually manage your emotions when you feel bad? What strategies work well and not so well for you?
- Is there a connection between the masculine norm and the difficulties with talking openly about suicidal thoughts? What can we do about it?

If you are contemplating suicide and feel bad: talk to someone, look for help among those closest to you, or seek professional help.

COMMUNICATION

We have now set up the framework that allows us to be vulnerable and open, and it is time to communicate and locate the pitfalls. There are tons of books with theories and thoughts about communication that you can dig into, but I have chosen to mention a few things that have helped me. If you want to dig deeper, find whatever suits you for the moment.

Seeing each other's perspective

What if there is no right or wrong? Communication is not a competition, and there is no winner. It is all about telling someone how you have experienced something and understanding how the other person has experienced the same thing. Allow each other time to talk and time to listen. Avoid the drama of entering a "parent role" and be reprimanding or a "child role" and flee. Talk about things with respect for each other. It is okay to disagree.

- How do you think that you generally communicate and talk about different things?
- How do you communicate with your closest family/partner? How do you communicate at work/school? In other contexts? Are there any differences?
- What do you do to see other people's perspective?
- What is most important to you when someone else is going to see your perspective?
- If you end up in an argument, what role do you usually take?

Talking about the little things that annoy you

I chose not to discuss small things that bothered and annoyed me because I didn't want to be difficult or get in the way. People could tell I was tense, but I didn't say anything. I now realize that I was unaccustomed to talking about these things; I was afraid of conflict and that someone would get angry. But what if that isn't so dangerous, what if the real danger is keeping a lid on these little things and letting them boil over? If anything bothers you, it means it is important to you, and you need to talk about it.

- How do you deal with little things that annoy you in your everyday life? Expectations, responsibilities, chores, etc.
- What is there that other people do that annoy you, but you choose not to bring up for discussion? Behaviors, habits, people asking for help or changing their minds, etc.

- How do you feel about disagreements?
- What are you afraid will happen if you disagree with someone and voice it?
- In what manner would you like to deal with and talk about different things with your family and friends? What difference would it make for you if you could bring up things in a better way?

Saying yes and no

I often said yes to things even though I didn't want to. I thought that the person asking should understand that I didn't want to. Or, I thought that if I help now then I will get it back later—that is, I added an expectation of getting something in return. But what if saying yes is giving, without expecting to get something in return? Otherwise, I will have to be clear about the fact that I am saying yes because I expect the other person to help me in return. And what if saying no is actually a yes to yourself and what you want?

- Reflect on how you think when you say yes to others. How do you feel?
- If you don't want to do something that someone asks or invites you to do, how do you tell the other person that you don't want to?
- What are you afraid will happen if you say no? Think about it—what would actually happen?
- If you ask someone for help and they say no, how does that make you feel?

Holidays etc.

Another thing about expectations has to do with family and friends, holidays and various events. I talked with my father about it when I went to see him, and we also talked about family holidays like Christmas and Easter. Talk to your family and close ones, because there are often expectations that we don't talk about but which create pressure, stress, and/or tension.

- How do you speak to your family and other relatives about your expectations about family holidays?
- What expectations do you think your family and other relatives have about family holidays?
- What do you want to get out of holidays? What is most important? What are your expectations?
- What would holidays and other events look like if you could control them according to what is important and reasonable for you?

RECLAIM YOUR LIFE—YOUR EVERYDAY STRATEGY

Doing new things and changing your behavior and habits can take time. It can be uncomfortable, and a lot has to do with breaking old habits. You break something that you are accustomed to and that brings with it a feeling of unfamiliarity. Be kind to yourself in this process; don't judge yourself but see it instead as a kind of learning. It is like a pendulum when you learn something new: you may fall back, but step by step you learn something that will increase your wellbeing. Other people might also experience unfamiliarity and discomfort if you change your behavior and your perspective on things. Give it time and understand that it can be difficult for them. But remember that you choose for you, so that you will feel well.

Time to yourself

During my pilgrimage, I talk about understanding how all of us did "our own Camino." That is, we were all part of the group but sometimes we wanted to be alone and there was nothing odd about that. In the past, I have experienced that I "should" be social and stay in a group and listen, even though I really wanted to do something else. Now I feel safe enough to take time to myself. I don't have to be social to be successful. If I don't feel like listening or staying put, it has nothing to do with the other person being uninteresting; it is all about me wanting to be alone for a while. Some people want to talk and be heard, and I gladly listen, but sometimes I just want to be alone.

- What do you think would happen if you chose not to take part in the coffee break or lunch at work/in school? What expectations do you think there are?
- What do you think would happen if you chose to walk out alone for a while at a social event, a dinner with friends, or a party?
- How would you feel if someone else walked out for a while or chose to leave early from a social event?
- How would you feel if you were given more space to do what suits you best in different social contexts?

Being available in the digital world

Always being connected and available stressed me out, even if I didn't notice it. It snuck up on me as it initially was fun that people could reach me all the time. But when I checked my email before I went to bed, it got my thoughts spinning about how I should reply. It would have been better if I had checked my email in the morning instead. All the stimulus from social media and being connected kept my brain running at full speed. The natural pause that I could easily find before I got a smartphone had disappeared.

- How do you use your smartphone and social media today? In what ways does using a smartphone or social media affect you? What are the pros and cons?
- What expectations do you have on replying to messages? What is the "rule" in your family?

In my experience, expectations and pressures regarding availability at work have changed. Several people that I have talked to feel that pressure—an email from the manager in the evening, and what should you do, should you reply? If you want to make a good impression, what should you do? Will the manager ask me in the morning if I read the email that was sent last night? Or, the other way around: At what times is it acceptable to send an email? Am I viewed as odd if I reply to an email at 10:30 pm? I believe there are many questions about this that remain unanswered.

- What expectations are there at your workplace regarding availability and replying to emails and messages? Have you discussed different expectations and rules regarding availability?
- Do you feel stress over the expectations on availability? If so, what would you need to make it better?
- Can you control and plan your day or is it often interrupted in a way that doesn't suit you? How would you like your day to be and how can you make it so?

Making your own choices—and letting others make theirs

I told you about how I talked to a therapist during my separation. She helped me see how far I had come on my journey and in my personal development. She also mentioned that you can't make choices for other people. You can tell them how you feel, you can contribute to their well-being, you can be there for them, but you can't make choices for them. They are responsible for their own choices and decisions, and they are grown up enough to have that responsibility.

- How do you deal with standing up for your own decisions, even if someone else is affected and perhaps disappointed?
- How do you want other people to act/respond when you choose for you?
- How do you feel about letting other people make their own choices even if it affects you?

Listening to yourself

We have now gone through a number of questions and you have been given a chance to dive deep into yourself. You have reflected on what you want to do, and what you need, physically and mentally, to feel well. You have gained a deeper understanding of emotional management and being vulnerable. You have reflected on norms and communication. Now, it is time to choose for yourself and start reclaiming your life.

- What do you take from these reflections?
- What will you do differently from now on?
- How has your opinion of vulnerability changed?
- What difference do you think that will make in your life?
- What will be your first step towards being more of you when you put down this book?

Let us dream a little

You have now begun a process towards being more yourself and letting others to be more themselves. We can now take the opportunity to dream a little about our future, our society, and our planet.

- What would it be like if your friends and family were more themselves?
- What would it be like at your workplace if everyone were more themselves and more emotionally safe towards others?
- What would it be like in society if the masculine norm were broken, if we were allowed to be vulnerable, and it were more okay to talk about how we feel?
- What kind of world can we give to our children?

CHAPTER 18

My Book Menu

The Celestine Prophecy, James Redfield

As I mentioned, this book got me to listen to my intuition. It is a great story if you want to follow the nine insights and follow your heart. It is all about talking to people about what is on your mind and seizing opportunities. It also speaks of how you can be affected by people you meet and how you handle conflict and drama that you are drawn into.

A New Earth:
Awakening to Your Life's Purpose, Eckhart Tolle

This was one of the "hippy dippy" books I didn't show anyone that I had read ☺ I read it around 2010. It is about separating yourself from your ego. Your ego can get stuck in things, stories from the past, pain, and so on—but it is not you. It is an interesting book with the power to move you, especially if you are stuck in things, or thoughts like, "This is who I am, and it will never change."

The Power of Now:
A Guide to Spiritual Enlightenment, Eckhart Tolle

Do you want to live in the present? Do you feel like you are always stuck in your past or your future? Are you stuck in psychological pain? This is a beautiful and elevating book that is also available as a series of interviews. Eckhart Tolle was interviewed by Oprah Winfrey and they talked about this book in several episodes.

Choosing Joy, Kay Pollak

This book deals with how you can change the way you feel. To me, it is all about sorting out my thoughts and viewing them with perspective. How do you choose to view your everyday life? What do you choose to practice and become good at? Do you want to practice being negative and seeing errors everywhere or do you want to practice choosing joy for yourself?

The Monk Who Sold His Ferrari, Robin Sharma

A modern classic in which we get to follow the lawyer who becomes a monk and comes back to help his friend. A book full of great reflections, and I can identify with the journey from being burned out and how I broke the "normal" patterns.

Paulo Coelho—all his books ☺

I have read all his books and can recommend them all. They are all great and sweet in their own way, and they fit different situations and needs. Begin with whichever one you feel like; you know which one you need to read.

The Real Happy Pill:
Power Up Your Brain by Moving Your Body, Anders Hansen

A book based on research that shows how much better we feel when we exercise. With this book, Hansen wants to highlight what modern science knows about the positive effects of physical exercise. How it helps children perform better in school, how it counteracts depression, and how we can avoid pills and still be healthy. That we create new brain cells and simply feel better with different kinds of physical exercise.

Reinventing Your Life:
The Breakthrough Program to End Negative Behavior
and Feel Great Again, Jeffrey E. Young & Janet S. Klosko

This book made me understand the patterns we create in our lives. How we can end up in destructive patterns and situations while we feel comfortable because it is something we are used to. The book gives examples of different life themes/patterns as well as examples of how to break these. It is a good introduction to understanding your own life patterns.

The Highly Sensitive Person:
How to Thrive When the World Overwhelms You, Elaine N. Aron

To me as a highly sensitive person, this book has been very important. It gives me perspective, I recognize myself in the descriptions, and I understand myself in a whole new way. Aron talks about different perspectives in which our upbringing shapes us and how that is expressed today. A very good book that I highly recommend, especially if you are a highly sensitive person, if you think you might be, or if you know someone who is.

The Journey: A Practical Guide to
Healing Your Life and Setting Yourself Free, Brandon Bays

What if you could break up and resolve diseases and emotions by venting your feelings? This is an interesting book that deals with how you, by diving deep into yourself, can identify things which influence the way you feel and act today. How you can resolve things that happened in your childhood but still affect you today. I have used parts of this theory to resolve a lot of things in myself, things I didn't know about but were limiting my life in many ways.

Rising Strong, Brené Brown

I read this book towards the end of my writing process, and it summarized much of what I have been going through on this journey. Having the courage to go out and be vulnerable, to open up and test new ground. It is all about falling and getting back up again. Brown has written several books and highlights the strength that comes from being vulnerable.

Being You, Changing the World, Dain Heer

What if you could be more you? What if you already are everything and just need to release more of yourself? This is a book for dreamers who want to view life differently. How can you let go of things and your old baggage? Create, reshape, and embrace more of life. How does it get any better than this? ☺